International Operations

International Operations

*How Multiple Environments Impact
Productivity and Location Decisions*

Harm-Jan Steenhuis

BEP BUSINESS EXPERT PRESS

International Operations: How Multiple Environments Impact Productivity and Location Decisions

First published in 2015 by
Business Expert Press, LLC
222 East 46th Street, New York, NY 10017
www.businessexpertpress.com

ISBN-13: 978-1-60649-578-0 (paperback)
ISBN-13: 978-1-60649-579-7 (e-book)

Business Expert Press Supply and Operations Management Collection

Collection ISSN: 2156-8189 (print)
Collection ISSN: 2156-8200 (electronic)

Cover and interior design by Exeter Premedia Services Private Ltd., Chennai, India

First edition: 2015

10 9 8 7 6 5 4 3 2 1

Printed in the United States of America.

Abstract

International Operations: How Multiple Environments Impact Productivity and Location Decisions provides a comprehensive discussion of the factors that affect international operations. International operations can involve sales and production activities. Companies are often too optimistic about the productivity of international sales, that is, overestimate the development of international markets. Companies are also often too optimistic about the productivity of international production, that is, underestimate the costs and efforts involved. This leads to disappointing results or divestment of international operations.

Beginning with a country level perspective, the discussion starts with an explanation of national culture and its impact since this is a basis for understanding differences in national environments. It then continues with discussing why governments are often interested in attracting international businesses as a tool toward economic and technological development. At the same time this illustrates that there are disadvantages for companies. Next is a discussion of the advantages of operating in international environments such as, among other things, potential consumer market development and access to lower production costs.

The discussion then shifts to a company level perspective by discussing different internationalization methods for companies, which includes a discussion of outsourcing, and what to pay attention to when considering an outsourcing decision. This is followed by a discussion of the appropriateness of different types of international operations networks and the roles of plants within these networks. The book concludes with a discussion of some of the challenges and costs involved when transferring operations technology and knowledge to a plant in a different country.

This book is written for executives and graduate students and provides many examples and practical insights to help them be better prepared for operating internationally.

Keywords

economic development, industrial development, international management, international operations, national culture, technological development, technology transfer

Contents

Preface

The international management literature does not typically examine the detailed level of operations whereas the operations management literature does not typically examine international influences in much depth. A much richer understanding can be accomplished by combining these different perspectives and, therefore, this book on international operations. At this point I would like to draw attention to a few items. First, many examples are provided in the book and many of those are based on personal experiences. As times change, so do environments. Therefore, in many instances dates are provided with examples and locations so that the reader can put this in the current context. Second, a lot can be learned by examining where things have gone wrong before. Hence, in many instances examples provide information on approaches that have led to negative effects on productivity. Last, to stay within the tradition of an operations perspective, the main concept of productivity has been applied in the discussion so that in many instances the effect of factors on productivity is explained.

CHAPTER 1

Introduction

It was some 30 years ago, in the early 1980s, and French car manufacturer Renault had international ambitions, particularly toward the large U.S. market. By 1983, Renault had purchased a controlling stake in American Motors Corporation (AMC) and jointly the first product, the Renault Alliance, was produced. Despite some initial success overall sales were disappointing. By 1987, Renault gave up on the United States and sold its stake in AMC to Chrysler. This American adventure is estimated as having cost Renault $750 million.

In 1996, in a completely different industry, the British Telecom (BT) Group saw potential in the, geographically close, Dutch market. Initially, it formed a 50/50 joint venture with the Nederlandse Spoorwegen (Dutch railway company). In 2001, MmO_2 was formed with BT having 100 percent ownership. Over the years, roughly $1.4 billion was invested but results remained disappointing. In 2003, MmO_2 sold its Dutch arm for $17 million, a staggering loss on the investments made.

In 1998 in yet another industry, AMP, an Australian financial services group, was entering the competitive British market through its acquisition of the Henderson Group. Less than five years later, after poor performance of its UK business, AMP demerged its UK operations. It accepted taking a $947 million write-off in the process.

A similar story, this time in the health supplements industry, started in 1999 when Dutch food group Numico purchased U.S.-based GNC for $1.8 billion. Numico was Europe's largest maker of baby formula and GNC the largest U.S. retailer of vitamins. Numico's adventure with GNC in the United States was short-lived; it sold GNC in 2003 to Apollo Management for $750 million, that is, a little over 40 percent of the original purchase price.

Regardless of the industry, companies may experience these situations. The examples discussed are in developed nations but it is not limited to that. China provides a range of additional examples. With a population of 1.3 billion consumers, China appears very attractive. But things do not always work out as several companies have discovered. U.S.-based Best Buy entered the Chinese market in 2006; five years later, after a lack of success, it closed all of its branded stores in China. Similarly, U.S.-based Home Depot entered China in 2006 and it also closed its stores in 2012 after conceding that it had misread the Chinese market.

Despite the often glamorous headlines of international expansions in good times, there is also a much darker side to doing international business. Many optimistic international market entries are followed several years later by disillusionment, a divestment, or a loss. Some of this has to do with customer preferences as provided in the earlier examples. But similar stories also appear when manufacturers have made operations location decisions related to the cost of production and outsourcing to cheap labor countries.

An example is Dell's experience in India. In the early 2000s, Dell decided to outsource its customer service call center to India. Wages in India are significantly lower than in the United States and many people in India speak English. In late 2003, after many corporate customer complaints about the service level, Dell moved its corporate customer support back to the United States. U.S.-based Handful, producer of bras, provides another example. Handful decided early in 2013 to relocate its manufacturing from Guangzhou, China, to Salem, Oregon, in the United States. Part of the motive for this relocation was the expectation that the company may gain appeal from customers as they weigh the value of low-priced clothing against the factory conditions that produce them.

The phenomena of moving manufacturing back from low-labor cost countries is known as reshoring or onshoring and many examples exist from recent years. In 2009, General Electric decided to move production of some water heaters back from China to Louisville, Kentucky. Increasing costs in China with lower labor costs in the United States due to a new labor contract were part of the reasons. Furthermore, the cost and complexities of inventory, the lead times, and the shipping cost were additional factors that favored a U.S. location. Caterpillar provides another example of a company that, when deciding on the location for a new hydraulic excavator plant in 2010, chose Victoria, Texas, in the United States for its location. Several excavator models were already produced in Japan and exported to the United States and this production was also moved to the new Victoria plant. Studies show that more than half of the foreign direct investments in foreign production operations are divested within 10 years of the initial investment (Benito 1997).

The purpose of this book is to gain insight into the broad range of variables that affect international operations and location decisions. *International operations are defined as situations where a company operates outside its domestic location.*

Of particular interest is the productivity of the international operations. This is because cost is often an important part of doing business internationally and cost is intricately linked to productivity. Productivity can be defined as the relationship between output and input that is achieved, that is, the real output and input (Veld 1992).

$$\text{Productivity}_{real} = \frac{\text{Output}_{real}}{\text{Input}_{real}}$$

In mathematical form, this can be rewritten so that it becomes possible to relate it to the norm, for example, what is expected or planned:

$$\text{Productivity}_{real} = \frac{\text{Output}_{norm}}{\text{Input}_{norm}} \times \frac{\text{Input}_{norm}}{\text{Input}_{real}} \times \frac{\text{Output}_{real}}{\text{Output}_{norm}}$$

where a comparison of the real inputs that were used with the planned usage relates to the efficiency of a process and the comparison of the achieved outputs with the planned outputs relates to effectiveness of a process. Therefore, the preceding can be rewritten to show how productivity relates to effectiveness as well as efficiency.

$$\text{Productivity}_{real} = \text{Productivity}_{norm} \times \text{Efficiency}_{real} \times \text{Effectiveness}_{real}$$

Thus, productivity is a function of the usage of inputs and the outputs that are achieved. In other words, the achieved productivity is based on the norm (or planned) productivity multiplied with the efficiency of the operations and the effectiveness of the operations. The effectiveness can be viewed as achieving the desired output, that is, doing the right thing, whereas efficiency can be viewed as the means necessary to achieve it or the use of inputs, that is, doing things right. When operating internationally, productivity is affected and this is through effectiveness changes or efficiency changes. Two examples from advertising in Arab countries illustrate effectiveness. First, Samarin, which is a Swedish remedy for upset stomachs, ran a campaign showing basically three pictures. In the left picture a man looked sick, in the middle picture the man was taking the Samarin, and in the right picture the man was smiling (Symons 2005, 66). Similarly, a laundry detergent company's advertisement showed a picture with soiled clothes on the left, its box of soap in the middle, and clean clothes on the right (Ricks 1995, 53). Both of these campaigns are not effective in Arab countries as they read from right to left, thus essentially changing the message of the advertisement. The earlier mentioned example of Caterpillar moving production from Japan back to the United States illustrates efficiency as the same output is generated (the machines are still produced, and still sold in the U.S. market), but the cost of doing so has been reduced by producing them closer to the market in which they are sold. Thus, efficiency has improved due to less resources being used.

International operations can take many forms such as exporting to international markets, but it also includes sourcing from international locations, or having a factory in an international location. International operations are a rather complex topic for a variety of reasons. One reason is that optimizing a domestic company is already complicated enough and when international locations are included in the equation, it makes it much more complex. Another reason is that there is not just one way that a company can have international involvement. Further complicating the matter is that apart from the many different ways that a company can have international operations, there may be (a combination of) different underlying motives for the internationalization such as gaining access to low labor cost (a cost motive), gaining access to an international market (market access motive), or using local technological resources (skills and knowledge access motive). Figure 1.1 provides a snapshot of some of the main ways and possible motives to have international operations.

International operations are in one form or another part of different discipline areas. For example, from a country perspective there is public policy that deals mainly with economic and technological development

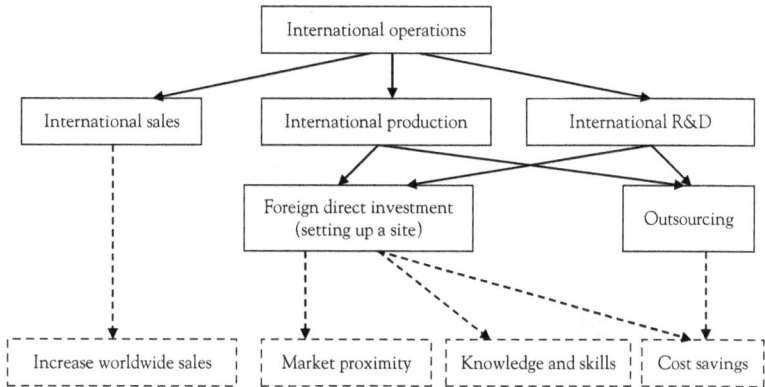

Figure 1.1 Some types of international operations and motives

and also economic geography that deals mainly with studying the geography or location and the spatial organization of economic activities such as related to clusters and the competitiveness of nations or locations. Together, these two areas deal with industrial policy and with the strategy of a country toward (manufacturing) industries. These areas are relevant for businesses because they provide insight into the attractiveness of locations. On the company side, some relevant academic areas are operations management, which is mainly concerned with how companies operate, and international management, which is mainly concerned with internationalization processes and, for example, trade. Together these two areas are relevant for businesses because they deal with a company's international and location strategy.

These different discipline areas are incorporated in the discussion in this book. Typical books on this topic start with discussing strategy, then tactics, and end with operations. In this book, a different approach is followed. The strategic elements can only be understood at the end because strategic decisions can only realistically be made once an in-depth understanding of the overall context is achieved. Figure 1.2 illustrates how this book is set up. It starts with a discussion of culture in Chapter 2 because culture influences many things. This is followed by a discussion of why countries may want to attract businesses. This relates to economic and technological development. Countries are frequently interested in companies because companies offer an opportunity for countries to improve their situation. From a more company-oriented perspective, Chapter 4

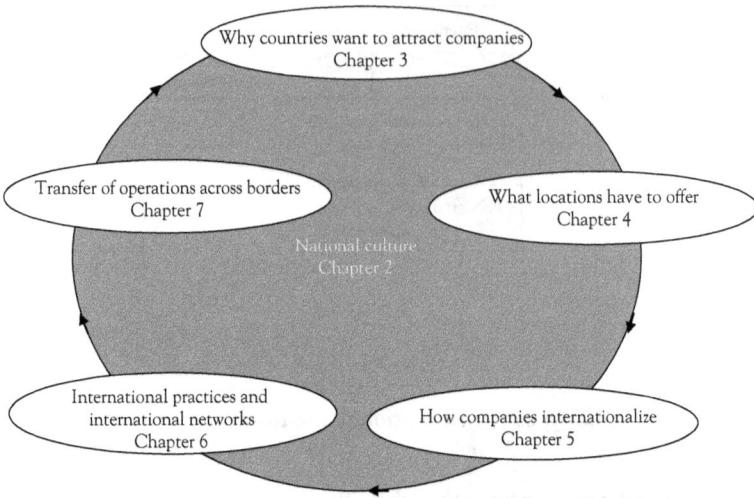

Figure 1.2 International operations

focuses on what countries have to offer. This may include customers, that is, markets, an opportunity to access lower factor cost, or the ability to access a skilled and knowledgeable workforce. The notion that countries are frequently interested in attracting companies to improve their position is an important realization because it reveals that the country has weaknesses. Companies should be aware of these weaknesses before getting involved and Chapter 4 provides advice on where to find this information so that companies can make a reasonable assessment of the situation. Chapter 5 assumes that international operations are a good option and then goes a step further to discuss how companies go about becoming internationally involved. There are many different ways that companies can get involved in international operations, but not all of them are equally productive. Chapters 6 and 7 deal with the next step in international operations, that is, working within an international operations network. In Chapter 6, the focus is on international operations practices and the configuration of the network, that is, the factories, where they are located, their role within the network, and so on. In Chapter 7, the focus is on the coordination of the international operations network, that is, issues of management as well as technology and knowledge transfer. Finally, in Chapter 8 conclusions are drawn.

CHAPTER 2

National Culture

It was some 20 plus years ago, in 1990. Until then I had traveled in several European countries but this was the first time that I traveled across the Atlantic Ocean to the United States. I arrived at JFK airport in New York City on a beautiful summer day and from there I was on a bus toward the hotel. This is where I experienced what could be characterized as a culture shock. The shock was the toilet. The toilet in the hotel, as are many still today in the United States, was a bowl that was filled with water. In Europe, I had mainly experienced toilets that had a plateau. I could not figure out why you would want a toilet bowl filled with water because any kind of *delivery* (loose Dutch translation) you had to make would lead to splashing up of the water. I found this uncomfortable. However, having said that, in the years following this I have talked to our American guests in the Netherlands who had the opposite reaction, that is, why have a plateau? And, what to think about my experiences in India with only two footsteps that you have to squat on, and remarkably no toilet paper but a faucet with a little bucket. I then quickly learned why when eating without utensils, which is the norm in India, would lead to frowning when I used my left hand while eating. The left hand, after all, was the dirty hand used for other things! In some Asian countries, people had introduced the modern Western toilet but residents were not accustomed to this resulting in practices that involved squatting on top of the toilet bowl. At times this led to slippage and falling into the bowl. Hence, for example in 2007 in Singapore, the National Environment Agency had a campaign explaining people not to squat on top of toilet bowls. Another example of a different type of toilet is the Japanese toilet. The modern Japanese toilet seat, that is, washlet, has an integrated bidet with control functions for controlling *shower hardness* and other features such as heated seat and warm water.

A different but related issue is the bathroom stalls. In my U.S. hotel room, I did not experience this but later on I discovered that in public places in the United States the level of privacy for bathroom usage is minimal. Toilet stalls typically have wide cracks between the door and walls, doors are fairly low and start fairly high off the ground. It felt to me as being very much exposed. Instead, in many European countries, public restrooms have maximum privacy. Doors go from floor to ceiling and there are no cracks anywhere. Once you are in the toilet stall, you are sealed off from the rest of the world, not even a fly can enter. Of course, there always are places that are worse than what I experienced in the United States. For example, in some Chinese locations it is still common to have a community bathroom where the only privacy that is formed is by the newspaper that you can hold up in front of you.

The point of this story is that when you operate internationally, many things are different than what you are used to from your home country. Even for very basic things such as a toilet, although you might assume that the usage is the same globally, you might encounter differences across nations. Another example of these differences in national culture is the debate in recent years in the United States about healthcare coverage and the availability of weapons. In many European nations, citizens do not understand why U.S. citizens are opposed to the healthcare coverage of all its citizens, nor do they understand why semi-automatic weapons can easily be bought in the United States. Differences in national culture have a huge impact on the different aspects of doing business. One of the areas in which this difference has an impact is on behavior when visiting another country. This includes behavior in business settings. For example, it is not considered appropriate to show the soles of your feet in Islamic countries. In Japan when handed a business card it is appropriate to accept it with both hands, not one hand as is typical in the United States. In general, there are wide differences in dress code, eating etiquette, and how to behave in meetings or public places. This chapter does not cover those aspects in detail because there are many books available on these topics. Here, the focus will be specific issues that relate to conducting business. Although it typically takes a very long time before an in-depth understanding of a national culture is achieved, the purpose of this chapter is to provide insight into how cultural differences may play a role in international operations through influencing, for example, the types of products that are sold or manufactured, the differences in manufacturing, and so forth. Some ideas are also presented on how to make initial assessments.

Understanding National Culture from a Scientific Perspective

National culture can be defined as the common elements that people in a society have due to being *programmed* by society. In terms of a metaphor, in a society everybody is wearing colored glasses due to their common programming. Suppose that everybody has green lenses. So everybody in that society views everything through these green lenses. Since everybody shares these same lenses, nobody thinks anything about this even though everybody has a green-colored world. When a person from this society visits another society where everybody wears blue lenses, this will be noticeable. To the person wearing the green lenses this may have not only the effect of noticing the other, blue colored glasses on other people, but also of becoming aware of wearing the green glasses.

Although some national cultural differences can easily be perceived when traveling to another country, it is scientifically a difficult concept to measure. Nevertheless, several studies exist that provide some ideas on how differences in national culture can be *measured*. Examples of different types of measurements for national culture can be found in Gannon and Pillai (2012), Triandis (1994), and Trompenaars and Hampden-Turner (2012). Perhaps the most often cited and used concept for national culture is provided by Hofstede (1997). Hofstede (1997) identifies four different types of manifestations of culture: symbols, heroes, rituals, and values, where the latter forms the core and the others are layered around it and can be detected through practices. Through his studies, Hofstede (1997) initially found four dimensions of culture, which was later expanded to six (Hofstede, Hofstede, and Minkov 2010). These culture dimensions relate to the differences in values that are found across nations. These values influence among other things interactions within a family, school, and, especially relevant to us, the workplace. The six cultural dimensions, based on G. Hofstede, G.J. Hofstede, and M. Minkov (2010), are described as follows:

1. Power distance: The extent to which the less powerful members of institutions and organizations within a country expect and accept that power is distributed unequally. Examples of high-power-distance societies are Malaysia and Mexico. Examples of low-power-distance societies are Denmark and Israel. In large-power-distance countries, the subordinates and superiors view each other as unequal, and based on this there is a hierarchical system. The ideal boss is a benevolent autocrat or *good father*. In these circumstances, an authoritarian leadership style is expected. A good example is provided by Triandis (1994, 183) who describes a Greek subordinate with a U.S. superior. The U.S. superior uses the participatory management style and tries to get input from the Greek subordinate while the Greek subordinate is expecting to be told what to do. The situation leads to many misunderstandings and the Greek eventually resigns because he cannot work for such a boss. Similar situations can be experienced when U.S. companies move production to Mexico because Mexico has a much higher power distance than the United States. In small-power-distance countries, superiors and subordinates view each other as essentially equal. The hierarchical system is just an inequality of roles, established for convenience, and roles may be changed so that somebody who is your subordinate today can be your superior tomorrow.

2. Individualism–collectivism: Individualism pertains to societies in which the ties between individuals are loose. Everyone is expected to look after himself or herself and his or her immediate family. Collectivism as its opposite pertains to societies in which people from birth onward are integrated into strong, cohesive in-groups, which throughout people's lifetime continue to protect them in exchange for unquestioning loyalty. Examples of collectivist societies are Taiwan, Venezuela, and Ecuador. Examples of individualist societies are the United States, Canada, and the Netherlands. Employees in an individualist culture are expected to act according to their own interests, and work should be organized in such a way that this self-interest and the employer's interest coincide. An employer in a collectivist culture never hires just a person but instead a person who belongs to an in-group. The employee will act according to the interest of the in-group even though this may not coincide with his or her own

interest. This, for example, means that for a company that establishes an international plant the hiring process may have to be quite different than in its own country. It should be noted, however, that there is variation within countries and that organization cultures can deviate from national cultures (Hofstede et al. 1990). Furthermore, while in collectivist countries hiring family members is frequently considered a good thing (same in-group that reduces risk), in individualistic countries, family relationships are often considered undesirable. In some companies in individualistic-oriented companies if employees marry each other, one of them will be asked to leave the company.

3. Masculinity–femininity: Masculinity pertains to societies in which social gender roles are clearly distinct (i.e., men are supposed to be assertive, tough, and focused on material success whereas women are supposed to be more modest, tender, and concerned with the quality of life). Femininity pertains to societies in which social gender roles overlap, that is, both men and women are supposed to be modest, tender, and concerned about the quality of life. Examples of masculine societies are Japan, Austria, and Venezuela. Examples of feminine societies are Denmark, the Netherlands, Norway, and Sweden. In masculine-oriented workplaces, there is a feeling that conflict should be resolved by a good fight and the management tries to avoid having to deal with labor unions. In feminine-oriented workplaces, there is a preference for using compromise and negotiation when resolving conflict. This means that if a U.S. company sets up a production plant in the Netherlands, the management of the plant will typically have to be different than what they are used to in the United States because the United States is more masculine-oriented than the Netherlands. For example, there are Dutch laws regarding mandatory employee influence in decision making (starting at companies with 50 or more employees) through works council. Many owners of U.S. family-owned businesses of similar size find this a rather strange concept. Another workplace difference is that masculine-oriented societies stress results and try to reward achievement based on performance while feminine-oriented societies are more likely to reward based on need. Thus, performance-based pay systems are unlikely to gain wide acceptance in feminine-oriented cultures.

4. Uncertainty avoidance: The extent to which the members of a culture feel threatened by uncertain or unknown situations. Examples of high uncertainty avoidance societies are Greece, Portugal, and Uruguay. Examples of low uncertainty avoidance societies are Sweden, Denmark, and Singapore. The levels of stress associated with uncertainty can be partly reduced through regulation. Uncertainty-avoiding cultures have more formal laws and informal rules controlling the rights and duties of employers and employees. They also have more internal regulations controlling the work process. The emotional need for laws and regulations in strong uncertainty-avoidance countries can lead to rules or rule-oriented behaviors that are purely ritual, inconsistent, or even dysfunctional. People from low-uncertainty-avoidance countries often do not realize that the emotional need for a formal structure can also be met by ineffective rules. In weak-uncertainty-avoidance countries, employees can show an emotional aversion to formal rules. In addition to that, employees in strong-uncertainty-avoidance countries like to work hard, or at least to be always busy. In weak-uncertainty-avoidance countries, people are able to work hard if there is a need for it but do not have the inner urge toward constant activity, that is, they like to relax.

5. Long-term orientation and short-term orientation: Long-term orientation stands for the fostering of virtues oriented toward future rewards—in particular, perseverance and thrift. Short-term orientation stands for the fostering of virtues related to the past and present—in particular, respect for tradition, preservation of *face*, and fulfilling social obligations. Examples of long-term-oriented societies are South Korea, Taiwan, and Japan. Examples of short-term-oriented societies are Columbia, Nigeria, and Egypt. In the short-term-oriented workplace, of primary importance are the results of the past month, quarter, or year. Managers and workers are also psychologically considered in different camps whereas in long-term-oriented cultures owners-managers and workers share the same aspirations. This cultural dimension also influences school results. For example, international comparisons of countries show that higher scores on long-term orientation are correlated with higher scores on both math and science in the Trends in International Mathematics and Science

Study (TIMSS). This has implications for the available workforce in a country and their skill set.

6. Indulgence–restraint: Indulgence stands for a tendency to allow relatively free gratification of basic and natural human desires related to enjoying life and having fun. Restraint reflects a conviction that such gratification needs to be curbed and regulated by strict social norms. Examples of indulgence-oriented societies are Venezuela, Denmark, and the United States. Examples of restraint-oriented societies are Russia, Romania, and Egypt. A prime example of Russia's restraint orientation was illustrated during the run-up to the 2014 Olympics. For the more indulgence-oriented countries, Russia's stance on gay people led to talks about boycotting the Olympics and athletes, and sports fans from these countries were torn between on the one hand their love for sports and on the other hand their reservations about Russia's stance. Exercising restraint also affects the workplace as it determines what is socially acceptable. This, for example, relates to hiring practices and what type of behavior to expect in a factory in another country.

Part of the difficulty with these six cultural dimensions is that they relate to deeply rooted values that are not immediately apparent when visiting another culture. One could use G. Hofstede, G.J. Hofstede, and M. Minkov (2010) to get insight into the values. When developing the dimensions and their scores, Hofstede (1997) used a formula so that the scores for each country varied between 0 and 100 although when countries were added later on, in a few instances they received scores higher than 100. Hofstede (1997) provides the scores, which helps with understanding the position of a country's national culture. However, some of these values are subject to variation, for example, due to organization culture influence. Another point is that what matters when dealing with other cultures is the *relative position*. For example, Hofstede (1997) provides the following scores for the power distance dimension: Malaysia (104, the highest score), Mexico (81), the United States (40), and Austria (11, the lowest score). Based on this, it is obvious that Malaysia is a high-power-distance society whereas Austria is a low-power-distance society. In addition, Mexico is among the top-power-distance-oriented societies whereas the United States is among the low-power-distance-oriented societies. However, if you are a citizen in Malaysia, then Mexico might appear as a low-power-distance society because it scores quite a bit lower on this dimension than Malaysia. Similarly, if you are from Austria then the United States might appear as a high-power-distance country because it scores quite a bit higher than Austria on this dimension.

Another model that is more practical is from Lewis (2008) who mostly looks at culture from a communication perspective. He distinguishes three types of cultures. Linear actives are task-oriented, highly organized planners that do one thing at a time, concentrate hard on that thing, and do it within the scheduled time period. Examples of countries with a linear active culture are Sweden, the Netherlands, the United States, and Germany (Lewis 2008). Schedules and appointments are very important in linear active cultures. For example, in the Netherlands by the age of 13 children are taught to keep an appointment book. Breaking an appointment is of course possible but certainly requires communication. Even if the king were to show up unannounced, someone would still be expected to confer with people from previously made appointments to cancel those. On September 11, 2001, I was staying in Cambridge in the UK. The world changed on that day and initially there was no travel to the United States. Obviously I could not go back home. Nevertheless, there was no flexibility at the hotel in Cambridge where I was staying. My reservation was until a certain day and I was essentially kicked out of the hotel, that is, strict adherence to previously determined schedules and appointments.

Multi-actives are people-oriented, talkative interrelators who consider reality to be more important than manmade appointments. They are not very interested in schedules or punctuality. They pretend to observe them, especially if a linear active partner insists. Examples of countries with a multiactive culture are Brazil, Italy, Spain, and Greece (Lewis 2008). An example to illustrate this comes from the World Cup Soccer. In October 2007, FIFA, the International Soccer Federation, awarded the 2014 World Cup to Brazil. In May 2009, the venues for the tournament were unveiled. Several new stadia had to be constructed. Since May 2009, there have been many messages from FIFA to Brazil essentially communicating how Brazil is behind schedule, not making enough progress, and so forth, and how Brazil needs to put in more effort. A *test* for the World Cup was the Confederations Cup, which was held in Brazil from June 15 until June 30, 2013. Six of the stadiums were used for the Confederations Cup. Frequently, that is, every couple of months, there were messages in the media about Brazil's lack of progress. By April 10, 2013, that is, a little over 2 months before the tournament, it was noted that only three of the six stadiums were ready and that construction was far behind schedule. By April 15, two of the stadiums were still behind schedule. By May 15, 2013, another stadium was finished and by May 22, 2013, all stadiums were ready. This is how multi-active cultures work. The more important or urgent the work becomes, the more resources get allocated. In most cases, work is done on time but it does not follow the schedules devised by linear actives. In April 2014, there were still many messages in the media again because not all of the stadia were ready for the World Cup. When the tournament started in June 2014, the stadiums were *ready*. That is, soccer games could be played and seating for spectators was available. Nevertheless, several of the less important aspects such as landscaping around the stadiums and roads to the stadiums were not completely finished but this did not impact the games themselves.

Lastly, reactives are introverted, respect-oriented listeners. They rarely initiate action or discussion, preferring to listen to and establish the other's position first, then react to it and formulate their own. Examples of countries with a reactive culture are Japan, China, Taiwan, and Finland (Lewis 2008). These three categories are more practical than Hofstede's dimensions because they are more easily identified, that is, quickly noticeable when visiting another country.

Working with people from other countries but that have the same culture is relatively easy. For example, it is relatively easy for somebody from Germany to work with somebody from the United States, UK, or the Netherlands since these are all linear active countries. Two good examples are two of the largest companies in the world, that is, Royal Dutch Shell and Unilever. Both of these companies have a long and successful history and are based on cooperation between the Dutch and the English, both linear actives. Working with people from different cultures is not so easy. Lewis found that when linear actives work with reactives the interaction is satisfactory, when multi-actives work with reactives the interaction is

Table 2.1 Part of the schedule

Time	Activity
8:30 a.m.	Registration
9:00 a.m.	Welcoming and opening address
9:30 a.m.	First keynote speaker
10:30 a.m.	Networking break
11:00 a.m.	Paper presentations
12:30 a.m.	Lunch

time-consuming, and when multi-actives work with linear actives the interaction is difficult.

A personal example can illustrate the frustrations that can arise. In 2009, I went to a conference in Malaysia. The schedule for the conference was provided ahead of time and most of the participants stayed at a nearby resort. Bus transportation to and from the conference site was provided. Part of the schedule for the first day is presented in Table 2.1 and we were informed that the bus from the resort to the conference center was scheduled to leave at 7:30 a.m.

Without knowing exactly where the conference site was located compared to the resort, based on this schedule, and from a linear active viewpoint, it can be assumed that transportation time to and from the conference site would be somewhere around 55 minutes. This is because the bus was scheduled to depart at 7:30 whereas the first activity (registration) was scheduled to start at 8:30, leaving a little time for getting on the bus and getting ready to leave as well as arriving and getting off the bus. An expected travel time much longer than 55 minutes would interfere with the start of the conference while an expected travel time much shorter than 55 minutes would mean that people would arrive at the conference way too early so would not make much sense either.

On the first day, I made sure to have an early breakfast and then walked to where the bus was going to pick us up. I saw the bus that was going to take us to the conference and entered it. By 7:30 a.m. there were three people on the bus: a Swede, another American, and myself. By 7:35, and without a change in occupancy of the bus, my thought was that either there were not a lot of people attending the conference, or participants were staying somewhere else. Neither of these made a lot of sense though because with the three of us, they could have just sent a car to pick us up. In any event, there was not a lot of movement going on, that is, the bus was not going anywhere. Slowly, every now and then, somebody else entered the bus. By 7:40 a.m. I started to develop a slight panic because the trip based on the schedule and my estimation should take around 55 minutes and since it was now 7:40 a.m. it appeared that I was going to arrive late for the first activity, that is, registration. Although I was not going to be the only one that was going to be late, this was only a slight consolation. By 8:00 a.m. my wife walked by and based on her gestures I could figure out that she was wondering what was going on since the bus had not yet left. By 8:10 a.m. I had another light development of stress as, based on the schedule and my estimated travel time, I was now going to arrive late for the second activity at the conference, that is, the welcoming and opening address. Another 10 minutes later, my wife passed in the opposite direction and again made gestures indicating that she was wondering what was happening. I had no idea either and it was stressing me out. The bus left at 8:30 a.m. From the linear active mindset, the best guess for arrival time was 9:25 a.m. With any luck we would be on time for the third activity, that is, the first keynote speaker. Note that over the last hour I had taken the schedule out of my bag many times to look at it and to determine when we might possibly arrive, what we would miss, and so forth. By now, I was also thinking that the trip was going to take somewhat less than 55 minutes—maybe 45 minutes or, if I was lucky, 40 minutes. This still meant that we would arrive late. However, this adjusted shorter trip time does not make much sense to the linear active mind because why then was the bus scheduled to leave at 7:30 a.m. instead of, for example, 7:45 a.m.? This type of contradiction was frustrating and stressful. During the entire bus trip, I was somewhat on edge because of the late arrival and how this would mess up the schedule. I kept thinking about how I would miss the registration portion and with the rest of the schedule completely booked, when I was supposed to take care of the registration so that I would receive the right papers to make the meeting productive. To my utter surprise the trip actually took only 20 minutes and we arrived at 8:50 a.m. There was still some time for registration! Since I was one of the first off the bus, due to my panic of missing the registration I was indeed able to register. While involved in the registration process, I kept thinking about the bus ride and could not figure out why they had not scheduled it at least 30 minutes later, that is, 8 a.m. In fact, 8:15 a.m. would have been a good scheduled departure time because that would have gotten us to the conference site at a good time for registration.

The welcoming and opening session started 5 minutes late. This was equal to 5 minutes of frustration. The audience was there, the speaker was there, then why the delay? However, finally the speaker started and when he did, I figured that all he needed to do was keep it 5 minutes short and we would be back on track. In fact, after about 10 minutes, the speaker seemed ready to finish and I perked up because it seemed that we were going to be back on the schedule after all. However, this notion was short-lived as there was a second speaker who was welcoming us. By 9:30 a.m. I was getting a bit edgy again because it appeared the speaker was not close to being finished and now we were cutting into the third activity of the day, that is, the first keynote speaker. The welcoming and opening address took an additional 15 minutes and was finished at 9:45 a.m. instead of the planned 9:30 a.m. Although the day had started late with the bus, the first scheduled activity had started only 5 minutes late but now we were already 15 minutes off the schedule. At this point, I was looking ahead and saw that the keynote speaker was scheduled for 1 hour but after that, there was a 30 minute break. Thus, if the speaker did indeed talk for the 1 hour he was scheduled for, the break could be cut by 15 minutes and we would be back on track with the schedule. From the linear active perspective, the break was about the only flexibility in the schedule. As soon as I heard the first words out of the mouth of the keynote speaker, I knew that this was not going to happen. This is because the keynote speaker was French. France is another multiactive culture. They do not care as much about schedules. At 10:30 a.m., I was therefore not surprised to notice that the keynote speaker was still going full-force and seemed to be far from finishing his keynote. In fact, at 10:45 a.m. (the scheduled 1 hour) the keynote speaker was still going. Now, it was a question of how much longer he would continue, and thus, how short the break was going to be. In other words, it was more or less clear to my linear active mind that the session after the break would start at 11:00 a.m., after all this is what was on the schedule. From the linear active mind perspective, the break could be used as a buffer in the case of small deviations from the schedule. The keynote speaker finished at 10:55 a.m. Hence, this meant a very short break, I thought. Maybe we could just go into the hallway, grab some coffee and go back into the rooms for the paper presentations, we could just drink the coffee while others would be presenting. It was, however, not to be so. To my utter astonishment, we were told that we were now going to have breakfast in another building. We all got up for the short walk. Now, this is like a nightmare to the linear active mind. This was not even *on* the schedule! Where did this come from? It would really mess up the rest of the schedule! And, apart from that, most participants were staying at the resort where we just had breakfast a little while ago, so why this breakfast? We spent an hour eating, drinking, and talking with each other. All this time, I was regularly glancing at my watch to see when this unscheduled activity was going to end and to assess the damage to the schedule. We finally got back to the other building to start the next activity, paper presentations, at noon, a full hour behind schedule. In these sessions, there were supposed to be three presentations of 30 minutes each, until 12:30 p.m. This now turned into three presentations of 10 minutes each so that we could have lunch at 12:30 p.m. I do not really know why we had lunch at 12:30 p.m. when we just finished breakfast at noon.

This little story illustrates the difficulties that linear actives face when working with multi-actives. For the multi-actives, they plan priorities not according to a schedule but they are more flexible depending on how important something is. They are also much more people-oriented and networking and socializing is considered important. For the linear actives, the schedule is extremely important. It is possible for linear actives and multi-actives to work together but it leads to a lot of frustration as they operate in different ways. Similar to the frustrations that I experienced in the preceding example, my French (multi-active) brother-in-law experiences the opposite type of frustrations when dealing with the tightly scheduled activities of the linear actives. How can you, for example, immediately get into business or cut somebody off just at some *arbitrary* point in time instead of working on the relationship first?

It is useful to make an assessment of other cultures you are dealing with when operating internationally because this will allow you to anticipate and understand where the other people are coming from. It will also give you a sense of how much time and work is going to be required to be involved in the relationship.

For example, if a company from a linear active country sets up a plant in or outsources to a multiactive country, it will have to incorporate in its plans the extra time needed for communications and direct supervision compared to if it was dealing with a company in another linear active culture. Because multi-actives operate more based on the importance of something, it is often necessary to have foreign expatriates on site or in frequent contact to communicate the importance of the work. Another insight in this was that, when visiting a Mercedes Benz plant in Pune, India, in 1998, I noticed that in the boardroom there were little signs on the large table with the *rules* of how to conduct a meeting. These rules made sense when considering the German linear active approach versus the more multiactive approach in India. They were probably designed to try to keep things orderly from a German perspective.

With these explained scientific viewpoints on culture and aspects in mind, let us now look at national culture from another viewpoint.

Understanding National Culture from a Societal Mechanisms Perspective

As mentioned previously, national culture can be viewed as how we are programmed by our society. This programming is the result of interactions that take place in society. This is, for example, not only through the sharing of values through parenting, through education, through communication channels such as TV, but also through laws and religious practices. These practices then are influenced by national culture and reinforce the culture as well (or lead to changes) (see Figure 2.1).

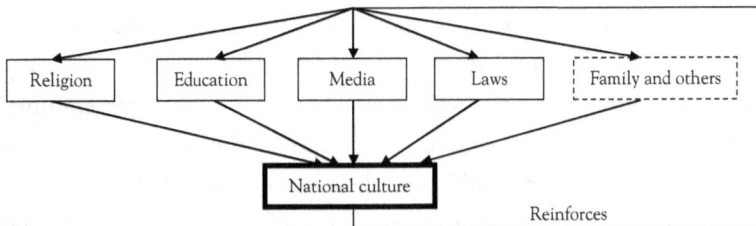

Figure 2.1 Culture and the programming of a society

Religion

Table 2.2 provides an overview of the presence of some of the main religions in some countries. It illustrates how some countries are overwhelmingly oriented on a specific religion, for example, Argentina (Catholic), India (Hindu), Israel (Jewish), Pakistan (Muslim), Taiwan (Buddhist or Taoist), while other countries have more of a mix, for example, Singapore and the United States, or even have a large portion of their population not having a religion, for example, the Netherlands. In contrast, not having a religion is illegal in Indonesia where citizens are required to declare a religion on, for example, their ID card. Note that not having a religion is different from being an Atheist, which is essentially a strong expression against religion. In Table 2.2 this is captured under *Other*.

The underlying values and beliefs of religions influence how societies operate. For example, in India there are many cows on the streets and inside companies there is typically a small shrine with a statue or depiction of a Hindu deity with flowers, beads, and so forth. This allows employees to practice their Hindu religion during working hours. Similarly, in Cairo it is quickly obvious that Egypt is influenced by Islam because during the day the call for prayer can be heard all over the city. Interestingly, the loudspeakers for this are incorporated into the surroundings. For example, there are fake palm trees with speakers hidden at the top behind fake leaves. Religion also has a large influence on what is considered appropriate communication and behavior, and it may affect the type of products

Table 2.2 Presence of religion in selected countries

| | Buddhist/ Taoist (%) | Christian | | Hindu (%) | Muslim (%) | Jewish (%) | Other (%) | None (%) |
		Catholic (%)	Protestant (%)					
Argentina		92	2			2	4	
India			2	81	13		4	
Israel						76	24	
Netherlands		30	20		6		2	42
Pakistan					96		4	
Singapore	43	5	10	4	15		8	15
Taiwan	93	5					3	
United States		24	51		1	2	18	4

Source: The World Factbook.

that are sold. For example, in some Islamic countries women are required to cover up, hence creating a market for clothing items such as a burqa and niqab. In non-Islamic countries there is a much smaller market for this type of clothing. Another example is that religious practices may prescribe acceptable relationships. For example, in many countries there may be guidelines on how men and women are allowed to interact. For example, in Saudi Arabia currently (2014) women are not allowed to drive cars. This affects their mobility. These types of rules also influence the workplace, for example, in male–female interactions. Another example is Islamic banking. An Islamic bank conducts its activities in accordance with the Islamic Sharia'h principles that strictly prohibit any payment or receipt of interest (Naser, Jamal, and Al-Khatib 1999). Business managers need to orient themselves on the specific methods that exist to comply with this while still earning money.

Education

Education provides another example of how people are programmed by their societies. To show some of the differences in educational systems and the values attached to it, I will provide some insights into the Dutch and U.S. schooling systems. Understanding how people are educated and in particular what values are reinforced is important for managers because these values ultimately affect the workforce.

The vast majority of the schools in the Netherlands are public schools. Primary school is for children ages 6 through 12. A large majority of time in primary school is devoted to learning the Dutch language and arithmetic with the remainder on topics such as topography, history, biology, and in higher grades English. Homework is rare in primary school, because in the Dutch culture they value playtime for children at that age. School is mandatory and being late or not showing up is unacceptable. It is very difficult, unless there is a valid excuse, like an illness, to keep a child at home.

In the system, there is no guarantee that a student will pass a grade. In fact, often children will not pass a grade. This is quite acceptable in the culture. It is also norm-based and standards are predetermined and rarely adjusted due to poor performance. Grading on a curve is an unknown concept and people would have difficulty understanding such a concept since it alters the grade and thus would not demonstrate the actual performance of students.

Starting with fifth grade, there is a process of continuous selection that results in students of similar ability being grouped together. In some grades, there are nationwide tests that play an important role for the child's future education. For example, in sixth grade students get four tests, that is, two tests on Dutch language and two on arithmetic. The results of these tests essentially determine where students go next.

After the sixth grade education gets more serious. In contrast to primary school, in secondary school there is homework and one aspect of schooling is to learn to deal with responsibility and keeping an agenda. This latter aspect has a lot to do with the linear active aspect of the Dutch culture. There is not one set of schools, and no middle school, but instead there are several different types, and levels, of education. Some of it is more practically oriented while others have a more theoretical orientation. Eventually, a distinction can be made with regard to three types of education. First, there is lower to medium level professional education, which is more or less oriented on learning a trade such as being a carpenter, plumber, and painter, as well as a car mechanic; hair dresser; and care-related jobs such as working in daycare or nursing. To complete this type of education takes four to eight years after sixth grade. Second, there is higher professional education which leads to higher level jobs such as more complicated jobs (engineers) or jobs with more responsibilities (management positions). To complete this education after sixth grade takes at least five years of secondary education and four years of tertiary education. Lastly, there is the more theory-oriented university education that traditionally led to what would be considered the equivalent of a Master of Science degree of well-known U.S. universities. Until a few years ago there was no bachelor's degree. This education is focused on more complicated jobs such as those developing new theories or higher levels of responsibilities (higher management positions). To complete this type of education takes at least six years of secondary education and another four to six years of tertiary education. After the university education, students can continue with a PhD (again typically a four year program that often takes longer to complete).

The Bologna accord changed some of this due to the international perspective. The higher professional education and university education now both provide bachelor's and master's degrees. Internationally, the higher professional education schools are known as universities (of applied sciences) although within the Netherlands they are not allowed to call themselves a university since that term is culturally still connected to a different type of school.

In the beginning of secondary education, students get a broad range of topics (regardless of the level of education they seek) including Dutch, English, French, math, history, geography, and biology. This is in the second year typically expanded to include German, Latin (depending upon the type of school), accounting, economics, physics, and chemistry. However, after that a specialization occurs and students focus on specific areas so that by the end of secondary education students have six or seven topics. Although these are the only topics listed on the secondary school degree, employers in the country know that students also had other courses. In the final year of secondary education, topic instructors give tests during the year, which results in a weighted average score for each student. At the end of the final year (May), students then take a national exam for their topics. This national exam has the same weight as the weighted average score they achieved during the school year, which essentially means that no student is guaranteed the degree until they have satisfactory results on these very high-stake tests. All students in the country take the same exams at the same time. The exams are prepared by a special committee. This means that individual instructors do not know what exactly will be on the exam and thus also cannot teach to the exam. In fact, if strange patterns occur, for example, high average weighted scores for students going into the nationwide exam but low scores on the nationwide exam, then this would be grounds for assessing what the particular school is doing.

Although the schooling system is characterized by continuous selection, it is not a system of competition. Students do not compete with each other for grades. Items such as a dean's list, well-known in the United States, do not exist. Sports are also not affiliated with schools or universities. Many children participate in sports but these are part of club-teams outside of the school system. While at universities due to the much more extensive availability of sports facilities, there are sports teams, they do not compete against other universities but in regular competitions that take place in society. Also, in sports, there is a place for everybody, that is, whether you are young or old, excellent at the sport or not, there typically is a place for anybody to participate. When soccer matches are played on the weekends you can therefore see teams with members well in their 50s. Most games in any of the sports are amateur games with no entrance fee for spectators. Soccer is the most popular sport but other sports that are popular and for which the Netherlands has typically good international results are field hockey, swimming, and speed skating. Except for a small portion, most of the athletes are not professional. Soccer has the most paid professional players although most will have limited salaries (below $100,000). The best players are often recruited in other nations such as Spain, Italy, Germany, and England where salaries are much higher.

In contrast with the Netherlands, the U.S. schooling system follows a simpler structure. Essentially, everybody goes through the same schooling system until the end of high school, that is, 12th grade, which is equivalent in time to the end of university preparation in the Netherlands. There is already a heavy emphasis on homework in primary school. After secondary school, there is an option to go to trade or vocational schools although typically students are encouraged to attend college. In the United States, there are many private schools that are often expensive to attend. These schools are available at all levels. Similar to the Netherlands, schooling in the United States is mandatory but it is easier to keep a child at home for different reasons and it is even possible to home-school a child.

The U.S. system has a broad orientation with many topics throughout the years that are not necessarily continued. In other words, it is possible in secondary education to do a topic one semester or quarter, discontinue it, and then pick it back up in another year. This is not the case in the Netherlands. The broad orientation in the United States allows students to become familiar with many different topics and to have a chance to find something that they like. In contrast, the Dutch system is one where over time more focus and specialization occurs. For example, when somebody studies physics at the university level, then the course work is essentially limited to courses on physics (and math) only. In the United States, especially for the bachelor's degree, the orientation is much broader. Although the specialization system means that students will know more about a topic area, a disadvantage is that it makes it much harder to decide to go for a less common profession. For example, with limited exposure to photography or sports in Dutch schools, it is much more risky to try a career in photography or professional sports. The implications of these different educational approaches is that, for example, in the context of hiring, a graduate with a *similar* degree in the Netherlands has more depth and specialized knowledge whereas the graduate in the United States has a broader background.

In the U.S. culture, there is a much higher (implicit) expectation that children pass a grade and it is relatively rare that a child does not. Since the Dutch system is one of continuous selection, it means that students of similar types of ability are generally in the same classroom. In contrast, the U.S. system with a higher expectation of going on to the next grade and without selection leads to a wide spread of abilities in a classroom. Grading is not nearly as strictly based on norms as it is in the Netherlands and, for example, in the university system instructors frequently grade on a curve. An example of this emphasis on norms in the Netherlands occurred in September 2010. Of the around 500 students signed up for a European law exam at the University of Groningen, only 30 passed. In the United States, the grading would probably have been altered with this type of result. In the United States, there are often also options available to do extra work to receive a higher grade and scores above 100 percent can be earned. In the norm-based Dutch education system this is not possible. With increasing accountability of schools, there is a movement toward more standardized tests with performance criteria but this is difficult to achieve. For example in the state of Washington the Washington Assessment of Student Learning (WASL) was introduced in 1997. In 2010, after disappointing results (low test scores) and much protest it was replaced with a new test, the Measurement of Student Progress (MSP). Furthermore, much more teaching to the test is going on. Note that under President Bush the *No Child Left Behind Act* was put in place, basically making U.S. schools responsible for graduating students, that is, if a student failed, it was the school's issue regardless of student ability or background.

A consequence of the approach in the United States is that quality is hard to determine and that there are differences across schools. This is in contrast with the Dutch system where *quality* in a sense is embedded through its selection procedures and by having everybody taking the same exams (6th grade and final year of secondary education). That type of testing is impossible in the United States due to its size. Instead, the differences in the United States come from school reputation and sometimes orientation. For example, in the United States a student can earn a bachelor's degree from a community college but also from a university. Either of these allows a student to continue education for a master's degree. Transferring between a community college and a university is also possible during early years. Tuition at the community college is typically lower but the ease of transfer is influenced by reputation. The same applies to universities, that is, a master's degree from a regional comprehensive university in the United States has typically a lower reputation than a master's degree from so-called IVY-league universities. For example, many universities in the United States offer one year MBA programs while Harvard offers a two-year program. Although the graduates are all MBAs, their knowledge and skills are not really comparable. The implications of these different educational approaches is that, for example, in the context of hiring, the overall comparison of student achievement is easier in the Netherlands because they have national norms whereas in the United States the quality of an educational program can vary widely and employers need to be familiar with the nature of the particular school a student graduated from.

In the United States, there is often a sense of competition in schools and, for example, at universities there are dean's lists and awards for the best performing students in certain categories. Sports are also connected with schools. There are also club-teams and sports opportunities outside of school but overall this system has a much more competitive nature. For example, if a student wants to be on the university football team, then he cannot just enroll. Instead, it involves try-outs, and so forth, to determine the level of the player. There are only so many spots available on a team so only the best get on it. Often this means you already need to have a history in that sport through primary and secondary education. Note that if successful, these players may have huge professional opportunities afterward. For example, in basketball if a player is really good, he can indicate that he is available for the NBA draft. This is an event where the NBA teams pick available players. Interestingly, in that instance the weaker NBA teams get the first opportunity to select a player. Wages for rookie players at that stage are somewhat regulated and vary from around $1 million to multiples of that depending on the order in which somebody was picked. It is therefore no surprise that sports is popular and well developed in the U.S. schooling system where even if you attend a high-school basketball game you probably have to pay an entrance fee. The implications of these different educational approaches is that in the United States there is in general more emphasis on competition, which often continues in the workplace, whereas in the Netherlands there might be more of a culture of collaboration. Also, in certain fields, such as sports, in the United States there are more professionals at a high level.

Another difference as a result of the education system is that the Dutch educational system, through its selection processes, prepares for different job levels, that is, depending upon the school that was completed the entry level job is at higher levels in an organization. In contrast, in the United States the degree more typically leads to a lower level job where promotion then occurs through performance on the job. This is important in the context of international operations because an implication is that if, for example, a U.S. company sets up a factory in the Netherlands, it cannot expect to hire graduates from higher level educational institutions to work at low entry level jobs. In addition, the pay is also expected to be higher.

What this discussion shows it that educational systems can vary significantly and that they are embedded in their societies. The meaning of education, the meaning of what it shows on the degree certificate, and so forth, has to be interpreted in the society's context. It also has implications with regard to hiring practices, pay scales, performance criteria, and establishing of societal norms with regard to, for example, behavior.

Laws

Another way that people are programmed by society is through its laws. The laws and the way they are upheld influence people's behavior, as well as the type of products that are in demand by customers. For example, when driving on U.S. roads you can see many large trucks. The typical heavy truck in the United States has a large front portion where the engine is mounted in front of the driver's portion of the cabin. When driving on European roads, you can also witness many heavy trucks. However, the typical heavy truck in Europe has a smaller front portion and the engine is mounted under the driver's cabin. These differences are mainly due to regulations, which in Europe restrict the overall length of trucks. This includes the cabin and hence having the engine under the cabin allows for more storage space in the trailer. Similarly, there are weight restrictions in Europe. The result of these types of laws and regulations is that the demand for products will be different. This again affects what type of products are produced and sold internationally. Another example of the same phenomenon is the recent (2014) legal changes in some U.S. states with regard to marijuana, notably Colorado and Washington. To some degree, the use of marijuana has been permitted in the Netherlands for a number of years leading to businesses such as coffee shops (where people can buy marijuana for personal consumption) but also growshops, headshops, and smartshops where they sell a variety of related items, for example, smoking accessories. A company that is very successful in the Netherlands may nevertheless face extreme difficulties in entering international markets due to different regulations and laws in other countries. For example, in Singapore, there are stringent rules concerning the possession of drugs such as cannabis or hashish that carry, above certain thresholds, a mandatory death penalty and for lower quantities penalties ranging from public caning to life in prison. Needless to say, the hashish industry has in this regard limited legal opportunities for spreading production through international operation networks. Another example from Singapore is from June 2010. At that time there was a front page article in the *Straits Times* newspaper about a graffiti vandal, that is, somebody had put paint on a train, and this was headline news for several days. In the Netherlands or United States, graffiti on trains is fairly common but in Singapore this is not the case. Punishment for this offense was a fine of up to $2,000 or jailed up to three years, and caned between three and eight strokes.

Media

Yet another method where culture is influenced while at the same time providing an influence is through the media. When visiting a country for a period of time one can easily see what types of products are promoted through the media. For example, while watching TV or reading magazines in the United States it is noticeable that there are many commercials and advertisements for health-related products such as medicine as well as for lawyer offices. The health-related products are related to the health-care system in the United States and, for example, the relative availability of many different types of medicine that are only available through prescriptions in other countries. Thus, manufacturers of, for example, allergy medicines influence consumers by promoting their products and making consumers aware of their products so that even when a visit to the doctor's office is necessary, the consumer (patient) can ask for a specific type of allergy medicine. In many other countries, this type of advertisement and commercial does not exist because the consumer (patient) does not have the same number of options for medicine available to him or her and instead much of the decision-making power lies with medical doctors. Similarly, the U.S. legal system offers many options for people to sue others. This can be for a variety of reasons including accidents. There is an incentive for lawyers to get engaged because in some instances there are very high rewards. This can explain why in the United States there are commercials for law offices on TV.

The media are also influenced by the public opinion as well as influence public opinion through what is broadcast and what is considered normal or acceptable in a culture versus what is considered not normal or not acceptable in a culture. For example, during Janet Jackson's 2004 Super Bowl halftime show that was broadcast in the United States, there was the occurrence of a *wardrobe* malfunction that exposed her breast for about half a second. This led to a lot of media attention and public outcry for such indecency on public TV. The TV broadcaster, CBS, was initially fined over half a million U.S. dollars but this was eventually overturned. In many European nations, people could not believe the public outcry for this event.

Selling Products

The products that are being sold in countries are also influenced by the culture. This is especially true for food items and clothing but other

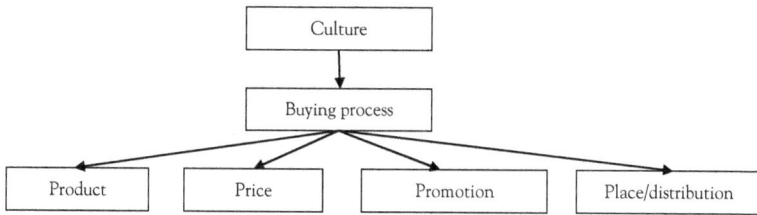

Figure 2.2 Influence of culture on selling of products

products are affected as well. It can be useful to think of this in terms of the marketing 4Ps, see Figure 2.2.

Product

In the preceding discussion, the example was provided of trucks and how U.S. trucks are different from European trucks because of differences in laws. Another example is washing machines. When comparing the U.S. washing machines to, for example, washing machines in the Netherlands (or other European nations), one immediately notices the difference in size. The U.S. washing machines have a much bigger capacity. Furthermore, a washing load in a typical U.S. washing machine goes a lot quicker than the smaller load takes in the Netherlands (20–30 minutes versus 1–2 hours). Thus, if you are a manufacturer of U.S. washing machines, you might expect market potential for these washing machines in the Netherlands. After all, a bigger capacity and a faster laundry process offer advantages. However, there are reasons why the washing machines in the Netherlands are smaller. First, there is the issue of space, that is, Dutch houses are typically smaller and have less room for a washing machine. It is also less common than in the United States to have a dedicated washer-dryer room. Second, there is the issue of power, that is, the United States has an 110V electricity system whereas in Europe there is a 220V electricity system. However, these two do not get into the key issue of the differences. The key issue is the difference in plumbing systems. In the Netherlands, it is typical to have only a cold water source connected to the washing machine whereas in the United States there is both a cold water as well as a hot water source connected to the washing machine. This means that in the Netherlands, once the laundry is in the washing machine and once it is filled with water, it needs to be heated up to the right temperature. The advantage is that the temperature of the water is fairly accurate for the type of laundry. The disadvantage is that the laundry takes longer due to the time it takes to heat water and the loads have to be smaller because larger loads take even longer and require much more heating, that is, a more powerful heating element. It is by no means trivial that a successful producer of washing machines in the United States has a realistic market in the Netherlands for the same products.

Another example is the use of color for a product or its packaging. For example, in many countries the color black is associated with death and funerals but in Japan the white carnation is associated with death. On top of that, as can be seen in sports events, some colors have a specific national meaning. For example Brazilian soccer fans wear the color yellow while Belgium soccer fans dress in red. This is not always connected to colors of the national flag. For example, Dutch sports fans can easily be identified in stadiums by their orange attributes although their flag does not have the color orange as part of it. Instead, it is connected with the royal family's last name, that is, Orange. These differences are embedded within societies. For example, the Sesame Street character Big Bird is yellow in the United States but the Brazilian counterpart is blue, the Turkish version is red and orange, the Mexican version is green, while the Portuguese version is orange.

Different demand characteristics are probably one of the most often underestimated issues in international operations, that is, export. Often, when a company has a successful product at home, it assumes that the product is also desirable for customers elsewhere but this is not always the case. In particular the food industry is susceptible to this. For instance, Applebee's discovered that its portions were too big and the singing of happy birthday songs was not appreciated overseas (Kleef 2010). But it also relates to nonfood industry items. For example, in 2011, I was visiting Jönköping in Sweden. While I was there I went to a supermarket. The supermarket had one very noticeable difference from any other supermarket I have visited. They used personal scanners. That is, a customer could sign up for this program and once they did, they had a Coop Shop Express scanner available to them when they went shopping at this supermarket. During their shopping, they use this scanner to scan the items they want to buy, that is, put in their shopping cart. Then, when they are finished they would go to a special cash register where the scanner was read, they would pay the amount, and their shopping was finished. This incredible productive system saves a lot of time because items are not scanned again at the cash register. How the Coop Shop Express scanner works can be viewed online, for example on you tube. However, it is also a system that assumes that customers are honest and scan all their items. At the supermarket they did random checks every now and then and so far it appears that generally customers are honest with this system. This system may work well in Sweden, but I am not so sure whether it would work equally well in other countries. This depends on honesty, the potential benefits from stealing (in an equalitarian culture like Sweden there might not be much need or benefit), and so forth.

Often people assume that what sells in their country would be appealing to people in other countries as well. Looking at it from the other side may make it easier to understand why this may not be the case. An example was already provided with the Swedish shopping scanner. Another example is the Tata Nano. The Tata Group is a large Indian company. They produce many different kinds of products including cars in their Tata Motors division. For instance, Jaguar and Land Rover are part of their portfolio. Tata realized that many of the available cars are relatively expensive, in particular for consumers in low-income countries such as India and so it embarked on a project to create a low-cost car. The result was the Tata Nano, which, although higher than originally anticipated, costs around $3,000. The Nano in this form is not available in the United States. Some of the consequences of the emphasis on low cost are as follows: The trunk is only accessible from inside the car; there is only one windscreen wiper instead of the usual pair; there is no power steering, no airbags, and no air conditioning; and the fuel tank is only accessible by opening the hood. Despite the low cost, it is questionable whether there would be a large market for this version of the car in, for instance, the United States where people are used to many of the features that are missing for the Tata Nano.

In conclusion, a product that sells effectively in one country may not be an effective product in another country.

Price

Another issue for manufacturers is that the price in one country is not necessarily comparable to that in another country and this is not always an exchange rate issue. Let me take General Motors as an example, and in particular it's top-of-the-line Chevrolet, that is, the Corvette. In the fall of 2010, a new Corvette C6 could be purchased in the United States for about $45,000. In the Netherlands, the same car was sold for almost €100,000. When the currency exchange rate of that time is added in, this translates to almost $140,000.* That is quite a difference in price! Thus, it seems that it might be a profitable business selling the Corvette in the Netherlands. The situation is a little more complex though. One product that could be viewed as competing with the Corvette is the Porsche Boxster. In the United States, it sold for about $72,000, which is significantly more than the Corvette. In the Netherlands, the Porsche Boxster sold for about €105,000, thus similar in price as the Corvette. This means that the basis of competition was quite different. Part of the reason for the higher Corvette price has to do with import duties, transport from the United States, and value-added tax. For Porsche, coming from within Europe, several of these costs are lower. In addition to the purchase price, a potential buyer also has to consider the cost of having and maintaining the vehicle. In the Netherlands, the taxation on vehicles like the Corvette is quite extensive. In effect, once you have a Corvette it is much more expensive to be able to drive and maintain the car in the Netherlands than it is in the United States. This means that regardless of the purchase price, the potential buyer for this type of vehicles is not the same as the potential buyer for this type of vehicle in the United States. With this in mind, it may not come as a surprise that the importer of Corvettes in the Netherlands, that is, Kroymans, went out of business in 2009. The point is that

---

* Similarly, in December of 2013 it was reported that the Porsche Cayenne's price in the United States was a little over $50,000 while in China it was nearly $149,000 creating a market of illegal imports into China, see *China Daily*, December 6–8, 2013.

whether or not it makes sense to sell a product internationally is only partly determined by the cost of that product. Typically when operating internationally there are additional cost involved, the marketplace may be different, and thus the basis for competition and the potential customer might not be comparable to the home situation. Even in instances where products from one country sell in another country, this may be for different reasons. For example, in April 2013 a McDonald's meal including a chicken sandwich, fries, and a drink cost Real 17 in Porto Alegre, Brazil. This was equivalent to approximately U.S. $8.50. Thus despite differences in average income levels between Brazil and the United States, the meal was priced the same in both countries. Several U.S.-based fast food franchises have established restaurants in many different countries that are fairly popular. However, while in the United States the popularity is due to the convenience of the ability to get fast service, in many developing nations such as India or in Eastern Europe, the popularity is one of image and status, that is, with the same price level, there is a different target market. All in all, what is productive in one country, that is, efficient or effective, may not be productive in another country.

Promotion

As was explained previously, promotion can be different in different cultures as well, for example, how medicine is promoted. What is effective in one country is not necessarily effective in another country based on cultural differences. For example, in the United States there are many food items for which coupons appear in newspapers for discounts. This is not as widespread in Europe. Similarly, the use of athletes to promote a product is different in different countries. A well-known athlete from one country is not necessarily effective for promotional purposes in another country. Furthermore, although using, for example, the openly bisexual Ireen Wüst (won several medals at the 2014 Olympics) for the promotion of a product would not cause problems in her home country, in Russia this type of an athlete's background might not be as effective for promotion.

Place and Distribution

The last issue for the product is how it gets distributed, and the size of the product. The amount of product that is sold in one package differs by country. For example, in the United States at a store like Walmart you can buy Shampoo in 3.8 oz (1 liter) bottles but there are also options to buy larger (bulk) bottles of one gallon (almost 3.8 liters) in size. In developing countries like India or Thailand, shampoo is typically sold in individual packages of 7 to 8 mL although bottles containing 160 mL are sold as well. This, obviously, is a significant difference from that in the United States. The reason for this difference is that in the poorer countries people cannot afford to have money tied up in large shampoo bottles and therefore prefer to buy the smaller-sized packages. Producers such as Unilever are well aware of this and have adjusted the size of their packages.

The same holds true for how the shampoo is distributed to consumers. In the United States, large retailers such as Walmart or other supermarkets are used to distribute shampoo. These retailers typically have several different types of shampoo on sale and for each type of shampoo they stock multiple bottles. It is not uncommon to have half an aisle at a supermarket filled with shampoo and related products. In countries like India or Thailand this is quite different. Although supermarkets exist, a large portion of the distribution goes through small stores. These stores are so small that typically customers wait outside and tell the store keeper what they want. Although, considering the size of these stores, they carry a wide variety of products, the number of competing products is typically low and there is also a limited amount available. Thus, such a small store may carry, for example, only 20–30 of the 8 oz. shampoo packages and 10–20 of the 160 mL bottles.

The same phenomena can also be observed when internationally comparing fast food restaurants. In the United States, the largest available size of a drink or French fries is larger than what is available in Europe and, for example, in Europe apple juice comes in 250 mL bottles, which is considered quite small in the United States. In 2008, at a Pizza Hut in Bangkok, a pizza with a drink cost approximately $12. The pizza was a small-sized individual pizza from a U.S. perspective although aimed at three to four people in Bangkok.

Conclusions Culture Influence on Selling Products

Culture affects the ability to sell products in different countries. What is desirable in one country is not necessary desirable by customers in another country. How products are distributed and their price points, as well as their design, may need to be adapted based on characteristics of the local environment.

Producing Products

The discussion in the previous section was oriented on the product. It is important to first understand how a product may have to be adapted to local circumstances when trying to sell it in another country. Once the necessary adaptations have been put in place, then the next issue to consider is how the product is going to be produced. Similar to a product, what is a productive, that is, effective or efficient, way of producing goods or services in one location may not be as productive in another location. Culture and its influence on particularly labor productivity is an important component but other factors play a role in determining the overall productivity of the production as well.

Many people have written about production in terms of production technology. For example, there is the distinction of hard versus soft parts of technology. One of the most insightful works on production technology has come from the Technology Atlas Team.* They divide technology into four components: technoware (object-embodied technology), humanware (person-embodied technology), inforware (document-embodied technology), and orgaware (institution-embodied technology). The influence of culture on production can therefore be viewed as the influence on each of these technology components, see Figure 2.3.

---

* The Technology Atlas Team and the individual members of this team were especially active in the latter half of the 1980s. The team consisted of people from different, mostly developing, countries who were primarily concerned with how technology could help a country's development, see for example Technology Atlas Team (1987).

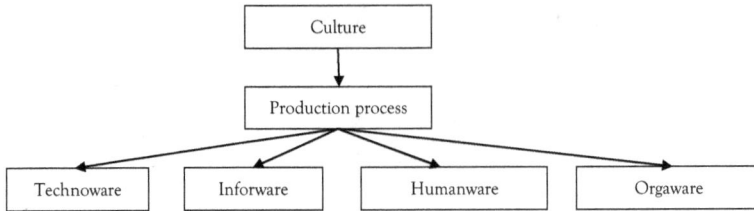

Figure 2.3 Influence of culture on the production of products

Technoware

Technoware is technology that is embodied in objects such as production equipment. There are several key issues that affect international differences related to productivity. One difference that affects the productivity of equipment in different countries is the climate of countries. For example, differences in levels of humidity may impact the productivity of machines. There may be more breakdowns and there may be more rust, or more maintenance may be required. Thus, the basis for cost is also affected. A related issue is the availability and reliability of electric power. For example, in many developing nations electric power is not as reliable as it is in Europe or the United States. Companies in those situations need to have power generators as a backup. Another difference can be the level of automation. In particular, in the case of foreign direct investment, a low level of automation makes sense when the argument is made that labor is cheaper. After all, when a process is highly automated with limited labor, it would not benefit much from low labor cost. Thus, when moving production to another low-labor cost country, it may be necessary to redesign the production process to a production process with less automation.

Inforware

Related to the previous discussion, when the level of automation is changed, this also means that the information such as documented in process specifications and process planning sheets has to be changed. Furthermore, different countries may differ in how they put information down on paper. This is particularly true for drawings. Computer-aided design software helps in this regard but it is still important to be aware of the different formatting methods in different countries, for example, what does a dotted line in a drawing represent? What do numbers represent? For example, on October 1, 1999, the *Los Angeles Times* reported that NASA lost its $125-million Mars Climate Orbiter because spacecraft engineers failed to convert from English to metric measurements when exchanging vital data before the craft was launched. A slightly different example of this is a European company that established a production plant in China in the 1990s. The company essentially constructed a new plant in China based on a copy of its European production plant. However, the quality of the concrete in China was not the same as that in Europe. As a consequence, its floors and ceilings had to be thicker than those of the European plant. Adjustments for this were initially not made in the drawings, which resulted in less space between the floor and ceiling. This was discovered when a particular piece of equipment had to be installed and it did not fit between the floor and ceiling in the Chinese plant.

Humanware

Probably the most important issue with regard to humanware is the productivity of workers. This of course is affected by their skills, which is affected by their formal education as well as on the job training. One issue faced by multinational companies in many developing nations is that once they train employees, these employees become more valuable and as a consequence have more and better job opportunities. Often, this leads to a high employee turnover creating a situation of retraining new employees, which adds cost for the multinational company.

When companies are considering moving their production to low-wage countries, they often talk about the labor cost per hour. However, this is only part of the story. The other part of the story is the productivity of labor, that is, how much the labor force produces per hour. A good discussion and explanation on this issue is provided by Van Ark and McGuckin (1999). The (average) wage in a developing country may be a lot lower than that in the United States but typically the productivity is also much lower, which offsets some of the wage differences. An example of this is the plastics-parts firm Cashmere, located in the United States.

By 2006, Cashmere had a hard time competing against especially Chinese companies due to lower production costs. It then embarked on a new strategy that took advantage of lower transportation cost for U.S. customers and a more sophisticated workforce. It invested in advanced manufacturing technologies that improved the labor productivity and allowed it to successfully compete against Chinese companies.

Note that from a nation's perspective, what also matters aside from productivity is the total number of hours worked, which can vary a lot, for example, in South Korea people work on average around 2,400 hours per year and in the Norway around 1,400 hours a year (Fleck 2009).

Orgaware

The last component relates to methods of organizing that has to do with (management) systems. Some of this is influenced by culture and not easily transferable to other countries. An example of this is the system of lean manufacturing and in particular the just-in-time portion of it. This was developed by Toyota in Japan. Many of its suppliers are relatively close in location and the system works well. But the system does not always have the same positive results in other countries. Obviously if in the United States a company is located in Seattle and has a supplier in Miami, the distance between the two is large. This affects the ability of face-to-face contact, which influences the development of the buyer–supplier relationship and shipping also may take longer than compared to some of Toyota's circumstances. What this means is that although the same system (lean—JIT) may be effective in another country, it may not have the same level of efficiency.

Conclusion Culture Influence on Production

Culture also influences production processes. Culture and climate can influence among other things the functionality of machines, the types of machines used, the level of automation, how production information is described, the productivity of labor, and how work is organized. A perfect copy of a production line in a new location will not necessarily achieve the same level of productivity as in the original location.

A Word of Caution on International Studies

By now it is clear that cultural differences, viewed in a broad way, have implications for doing international business. Students of business have to be careful about the cultural context of the materials that they study. Thus, for example, human resource management techniques that are taught and promoted in the United States may not be the most productive in other nations. This has broad implications and means that we have to be careful about generalizing findings of studies on management. In fact, it goes much farther than that and goes as far as understanding how people behave. Many of the currently established theories are based on studies in western societies and much of those were conducted with students as the participants of the study. It has been demonstrated that these theories are not universal and that, for example, ideas on fairness are not the same in different cultures—see, for example, Waiters (2013) where the work of Joe Henrich and colleagues on this issue is discussed.

An additional complication of the cultural differences is that they also influence how participants fill in a survey. In surveys, there can be something like extreme response style (tendency to use the endpoints of the answer scale) and something like acquiescence response style (tendency of the respondents to agree with the items). Studies have shown that this differs internationally (Harzing 2006). For example, the occurrence of extreme response style is less in Asian countries (Dolnicar and Grun 2007). This means that, for example, results of marketing studies to measure the market potential of products have to be cautiously interpreted because the responses for such a study may be biased based on a country's culture. It also means that any survey-based management study, including those that look at cultural differences, that reports on international differences has to be cautiously interpreted. There may be differences but part of the differences, or lack thereof, may be caused by a cultural bias in how surveys are answered.

Estimating the Impact of National Culture on Production Operations

This chapter has shown that national culture can have a big influence on a company's international operations. The main point to take away is that awareness of national culture differences can help managers to make better informed international operation decisions related to both products and production processes. This section will focus on the production processes. For products, several important aspects were pointed out in this chapter concerning the international appeal and acceptability of products and differences in buying processes. It is recommended to involve local consultants to conduct market feasibility studies. To gain insight and sensitivity in the influence of national culture on production processes, a manager can do the following:

- First, it is important to understand how the domestic production processes have been embedded in, and therefore have been influenced by, the domestic culture. To determine this, it is necessary to gain in-depth insight into national culture dimensions. This chapter has provided some basics but it is recommended to gain more in-depth insight through studying in particular the works by G. Hofstede, G.J. Hofstede, and M. Minkov (2010), as well as Lewis (2008). Then, the manager needs to determine how national culture has influenced production processes through the underlying national cultural values. This relates in particular to what is valued or emphasized in the culture, for example, how managers function and communicate, as well as how employees function and how the production process was designed.

- Next, the manager needs to map the national culture of the international location and how this differs from the domestic national culture. This means assessing which national culture values are different and by how much they are different. This can be estimated based on the dimensions by G. Hofstede, G. J. Hofstede, and M. Minkov (2010) or the types of cultures by Lewis (2008).

- Once the national culture of the domestic location as well as the international location is understood and their differences are identified, the impact of these differences on the production process needs to be estimated and a plan for dealing with this impact needs to be formulated. This can be accomplished by analyzing the four components of technology. For example, if a production process is moved from the United States to Mexico, then one of the cultural values that will impact the management of the human resources in the production process is the power distance. A plan for adjusting to the higher power distance of the Mexicans might require additional training of U.S. managers or another possible alternative could be using Mexican managers who get training in the U.S. plant to understand the production processes. Another example might be that the information needs to be reformatted and presented in a different language.

- Lastly, the cost of the impact of national culture needs to be estimated. Costs that might be included are the cost of production downtime due to religious activities, the cost for lower productivity due to management difficulties, the cost for cultural training of managers, which includes their travel cost, the cost of translating documents, and so on.

Estimating the impact of national culture on production operations is necessary and important because it provides a first glimpse at the true cost of having international operations.

Conclusion

Understanding culture is the foundation of any type of success with international operations. This is because culture and its underlying dimensions are often the explanation of differences that occur when operations become international. Understanding culture is not an easy task and deriving consequences from a business point of view based on this understanding is even more difficult. There is quite an abundance of research on national cultures but part of the challenge with this is the perceptions and who holds them. Really valuable insights can come from people with extensive exposure to different national cultures. Based on my own experiences, it takes about a decade to develop a really good understanding of another culture. Many aspects can be noticed earlier but to understand the roots of where the cultural stance comes from requires quite some time.

The initial focus in this chapter was on discussing some of the current theories on culture. These are helpful because they provide a framework with which we can start to understand cultural differences and also how to measure these differences or how we can become sensitive to perceiving them. The chapter then discussed societal mechanisms and how a nation's culture is formed and maintained through religion, education, media laws, family, and so on. This means that national culture has the potential to change. These societal mechanisms provide important clues to get an idea of the culture of a nation and some of these are more easily identifiable, even when visiting a nation for a short time period. National cultures can change over time. Values of a population can change due to immigration (ethnicity changes) as well as generation changes, and so on. Nevertheless, as stated by G. Hofstede, G.J. Hofstede, and M. Minkov (2010, 39): "The national dimension scores (or at least their relative positions) have remained as valid in the year 2010 as they were around 1970, indicating that they describe relatively enduring aspects of these countries' societies."

Lastly, I described how culture can influence the potential market for exports as well as how culture can influence the production process. Culture, in this regard, influences the productivity of international operations whether exporting, producing internationally, or when using other forms of international activities. Companies frequently make changes in product or process in anticipation of differences. However, a word of caution is necessary in this regard because Szulanski and Jensen (2006) found that presumptive adaptation does not work. This is because it is often not well understood what appeals to the customer. Making changes before feedback is received might be detrimental because maybe things have changed that should not have been changed.

Dealing with different cultures, for example, between linear active and multiactive cultures, is often time-consuming and can be frustrating. When engaging in international operations, the cultural aspect from a communications perspective, which is often ignored, has to be analyzed in an early stage as well as it involves, for example, the amount of time required for supervision and communication.

CHAPTER 3

Country Development and Attracting Business

About 500 years ago, the Portuguese established themselves in what is nowadays called Malaysia. Since that time the Dutch had it as their colony but more recently from the eighteenth to the twentieth century, Malaysia fell under British rule. During the Second World War it was occupied by Japan. Singapore had a similar history and had its period of falling under the British rule and was occupied by the Japanese. In 1948, the Federation of Malaya was formed, which became independent in 1957. In 1963, this Federation of Malaya with among others Singapore formed Malaysia. However, Singapore was not part of Malaysia for very long. In 1965, Singapore became independent. Singapore had little going for it. It had a past with some trade in rubber and tin and it had a relatively good location that had been used as a trading hub. Other than that, it had very limited resources and did not appear to have any particular advantages. To put this in perspective, Singapore's independence was about three years after the United States sent Ranger 4 to the moon. In other words, the United States at that time was already technologically advanced. The future for Singapore looked rather bleak. How was the new government, with these circumstances, supposed to improve life for its citizens? Malaysia had plenty of natural resources to build upon. Another neighbor with a similar history, that is, Indonesia, also had many natural resources. But with a lack of natural endowments, Singapore somehow had to transform itself. With the challenges being clear, Singapore's new government set out on a road to economic development. During the 1970s and 1980s, it used government control to guide the country toward more economic prosperity. Singapore experimented with import-substitution as well as export-led economic strategies. Attracting foreign businesses to invest in Singapore was a key part of Singapore's economic strategy.

By the early 1990s, Singapore's government published a plan for long-term national development, which it called the Next Lap. One of the goals was to achieve a per capita standard of living comparable to the United States by 2030. Considering the recent history of Singapore and the United States one might consider this goal preposterous. However, given enough time, that is, with about four decades to go, it might be feasible. Within a decade, that is, by 1998, Singapore was ranked as the most competitive nation in the world (Schwab et al. 1999). By 2012, the U.S. GDP per capita was $51,749 while that of Singapore was $51,709. The well-endowed neighbors, that is, Malaysia and Indonesia, were at $10,432 and $3,557, respectively.*

The development story of Singapore is remarkable in itself but even more so when placed in the context of development of other countries such as Malaysia and Indonesia. There are several ways of looking at the development of a country. For example, the United Nations annually publishes their human development report,[†] there are also reports that look at the happiness of countries[‡] and social progress,[§] while some studies look at social development (Morris 2010). The purpose of this chapter is to take a more economic viewpoint and to provide insight into economic development strategies, technological development strategies, the role of business, and how it relates to productivity.

Economic Development

Many countries, both developing and developed, have plans for economic development. For example, countries such as India, Indonesia, and China publish five-year plans with the goals for development. Countries can go about this in many different ways as is shown by Vietor (2007). The importance of business for economic development will be discussed in this section.

---

* This is based on World Bank data, see http://data.worldbank.org/indicator/NY.GDP.PCAP.CD
[†] See: http://hdr.undp.org/en
[‡] See: http://www.happyplanetindex.org/
[§] See: http://www.socialprogressimperative.org/

General Theory about Economic Development

After thousands of years without economic growth, the first country in the world that showed some economic growth was the Netherlands around 1750. Not long after that, the UK followed due to the industrial revolution (Bernstein 2004). Using the GDP per capita as an indicator,[*] Danielmeyer (1997) tracked the economic development of all countries over time and found that the upper bound of all economic growth curves is a nearly pure exponential[†] with a growth rate of 1.3 percent per annum (see Figure 3.1).

Dependent upon the starting point of economic growth for a country, it can grow faster than the growth of the upper boundary because it can copy what other countries have done to close the gap with the upper boundary. To say it differently, countries that are currently closer to the bottom in this graph have essentially the largest potential because not only is there a big gap between them and the upper boundary, but they also have the potential for much faster economic growth because they can learn from the more advanced nations—hence, for instance, the identification of large potential

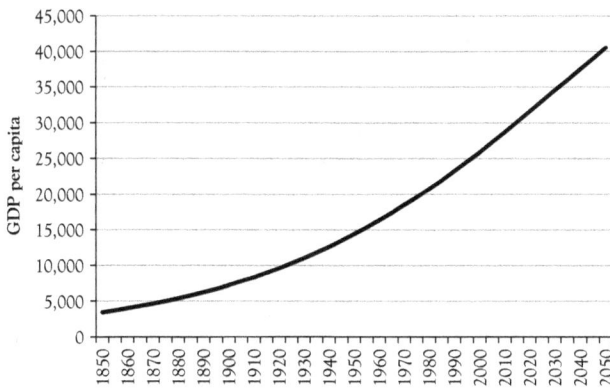

Figure 3.1 Development of the industrial society

Source: Adapted from Danielmeyer (1997).

---

[*] This type of historical data for different regions in the world can be found in Mitchell (2007a, 2007b, 2007c) or Maddison (2006).

[†] The pattern of data that Danielmeyer (1997) found has one other explanation, that is, that of an S-curve. This symmetric curve would have the year 2040 as the half-time of the upper bound's final height step.

markets in Brazil, Russia, India, and China (O'Neill 2011), as well as the Arab world (Mahajan 2012) and the African continent (Mahajan 2009; Radelet 2010). These locations are economically developing and have large amounts of consumers with increasing purchase power. In addition to this, companies from these countries are also growing and becoming more prominent. For example, the percentage of global Fortune 500 companies from developing countries is steadily increasing. The 2013 Global Fortune 500 included among others the Sinopec Group China (number four) and China National Petroleum (number five) from China, Petrobas (number 25) from Brazil, Pemex (number 36) from Mexico, PDVSA (number 38) from Venezuela, PTT (number 81) from Thailand, and Indian Oil (number 88) from India.

Different methods exist to measure where a country is economically speaking. For example, the World Bank classifies countries in four groups based upon the gross national income (GNI) per capita. This is illustrated in Table 3.1

The classification of an economy is essentially a reflection of the ability of a country to generate income. This is related to how productive the country is, or rather, its employment base. The more productive the workforce in a country, the higher the level of prosperity. In order for a country to *start* their path of economic growth, or in other words to improve its productivity levels, certain conditions have to be met. It has been found that, for example, property protection, scientific rationalism, capital markets, fast and efficient communication and transportation (Bernstein 2004), competition, medicine, the consumer society, and work ethic (Ferguson 2011) play a role. This is because these types of factors help with improving productivity. For instance, if there is no property protection, then there is little incentive for people to make improvements

Table 3.1 Classification of economies adapted from the World Bank (2013)

Classification of economy	GNI per capita in 2012
Low-income economy	≤ $1,035
Lower-middle-income economy	> $1,035 but ≤ $4,086
Upper-middle-income economy	> $4,086 but < $12,616
High-income economy	≥ $12,616

in their productivity. If, however, there is property protection, then the people have an incentive to, for example, improve their harvest from their land or to use patents because they can expect to gain benefits, that is, generate more income.

Economic Strategies

Three stages of development can be identified: factor-driven, investment-driven, and innovation-driven (Porter 1990). Identifying these stages helps to understand the process of upgrading an economy in terms of prosperity. According to Porter (1990, 544):

> Economic prosperity depends upon the productivity with which national resources are employed. The level and growth of the productivity are a function of the array of industries and industry segments in which a nation's firms can successfully compete, and the nature over time of the competitive advantages achieved in them. Economies progress by upgrading their competitive positions, through achieving higher-order competitive advantages in existing industries and developing the capability to compete successfully in new, high-productivity segments and industries.

Factor-driven stage countries derive their advantage mainly from basic factors of production. That is, for example, natural resources such as soil and climate in agriculture, or an abundant and inexpensive semiskilled labor pool. In this stage, a nation's indigenous firms compete solely on the basis of price and in industries that require little product or process technology or on technologies that are cheap, widely available, and sourced from other nations (Porter, 1990). Foreign firms play a role in factor-driven economies because they can provide product and process technologies, access to foreign markets, and employment opportunities. In the section Input Conditions in Chapter 4, I will discuss how the type of economy, such as factor-driven, relates to productivity. The factor-driven economy is sensitive to world economic cycles and exchange rates because they influence demand and relative price. The factor-driven economy is also sensitive for the loss or depletion of a factor condition, for example, labor becoming more expensive or depletion of available minerals. This has been occurring in China. For instance, in 2010, after several suicides of workers because of low wages, Foxconn Technology raised its wages. Other international companies such as Honda have also raised wages.

One consequence of this type of economic upgrading with increasing wages is that it makes the country less appealing for companies who are mainly competing on low cost factors. For example, van Liemt (1992) provides the description of several industries and how they have moved to other locations over time. Gereffi (1999) also provides a good illustration. He studied the changes in the textile industry by looking at where U.S. apparel imports were coming from. Over a period of a decade, that is, from 1986 to 1996, there were many changes. For example, China, Mexico, and the Dominican Republic became more important sources from where textile imports were originating. South Korea, Taiwan, and Hong Kong were countries that became less important as a source where imports were originating from. Another country-specific example is Taiwan. It is estimated that in the 1990s some 12,000 Taiwanese small and medium-sized enterprises (SMEs) moved, in particular labor-intensive, production, such as shoe manufacturing, to China. This was because due to increasing wages and an appreciation of the New Taiwan dollar against the U.S. dollar, Taiwan had lost their advantage in competing with emerging developing countries such as Thailand, Indonesia, the Philippines, and China (Hsiung 1998).

The textile and shoe-manufacturing industries can be considered footloose. Footloose companies have limited dependency upon proximity to specialized resources and markets (Premus 1982). This type of industry has a lot of freedom in locating where it desires and thus, for instance for textiles, when driven by low-labor cost, if wages or other cost increase in one location, they tend to move to another location that offers lower costs.

Many nations never move beyond the factor-driven stage. A crucial ability to move to the next, investment-driven, stage is the ability to not just absorb foreign technology but to improve upon foreign technology. The competitive advantage for nations in the investment-driven stage is based on the ability of the nation and its firms to invest in efficient facilities with the best globally available technologies that help improve the overall productivity. Firms compete with more complex foreign product and process technologies that allow competing in more sophisticated industries. The workforce becomes increasingly skilled. Basic factor conditions still play an important role but more sophisticated technologies, a higher level of local competition, and improvements in education, research, infrastructure, and so forth, allow for productivity improvements that in turn lead to increasing wages. Having a large home market can help with the development of local companies. At this stage, the country loses in the more price-sensitive industries but becomes more diversified in other industries and it becomes less sensitive to global shocks and exchange rate fluctuations. Governments at this stage play an important role by making investments, encouraging domestic rivals and rivalry, influence the acquisition of foreign technology, setting policies on, for example, foreign direct investment and trade, and in general by creating and upgrading the environment that allows higher productivity levels (Porter, 1990). For example, while I was visiting South Africa in 2010, compared with India (of the 1990s) it was noticeable that South Africa had many foundation elements in place such as roads, airports, and so forth. Where it still needed more work is in improving the overall labor productivity and, for example, having more, higher value-added, production.*

In the innovation-driven stage, there is a broad mix of industries in which the country's firms are able to successfully compete based on productivity due to high skills and advanced technology rather than on low factor costs. Conditions that help to push innovation and to achieve high productivity are sophisticated domestic demand, there are well-developed local suppliers and related industries, firms have sophisticated management, and the factor conditions such as the workforce are upgraded. At this stage technologies are created rather than simply acquired and improved upon. This stage is the most resistant to macroeconomic fluctuations and exogenous events such as changes in cost or exchange rate, because competition is based on technology and differentiation. Much of

---

* However, in recent years I have also visited the Langa, Shebeen, and Khayelitsha townships near Cape Town. During the apartheid years, people from District Six in Cape Town were moved to these townships and the conditions in these townships are still very poor.

the improvements have to come from the private sector but the government can indirectly provide ways for stimulation. For example, the government can stimulate the development of new businesses, innovative activities, the creation of more advanced factors, improving the quality of the overall business environment that also attracts businesses, and so forth. For example, in the IT-field, many U.S. companies have set up R&D facilities in Taiwan because it provides an attractive, competitive location, compared to the United States. Connected to this, governments can also pursue the development of clusters.

There is much debate about clusters and their definition, see, for example, Asheim, Cooke, and Martin (2006). Here, I will use the definition from Porter (2008, 215): clusters are a geographically proximate group of interconnected companies and associated institutions in a particular field, linked by commonalities and complementarities. Clusters offer several economic benefits such as enabling higher productivity, offering possibilities for companies and research institutions to build connections to better learn and innovate, and business formation tends to be higher in clusters (Ketels and Memedovic 2008). For example, Indonesia has applied a form of cluster policy to help develop its indigenous car manufacturing industry. In this case, Japanese companies have played an important role to transfer successful practices (Irawati and Charles 2010). Part of the difficulty with developing or encouraging cluster development relates to how integrated the industry is, that is, how many other industries is it connected to and that need to be in place. Aircraft manufacturing can be considered an integrated industry. This means that to develop aircraft requires many technologies across many different industries such as related to materials, wing design, aviation electronics, engines, and so forth. Initially software development was more of an island industry, which means less dependent upon the overall industrial environment. This is also related to the concept of industrial commons that will be discussed later in this chapter. This explains why a country like India can have a relatively competitive position in software development while it has many difficulties with developing its aviation industries (Steenhuis and de Bruijn 2004a).

Governments can follow many different economic strategies and these economic strategies consist of many different economic policies on topics including but not limited to fiscal deficits, public expenditure priorities, tax reform, interest rates, exchange rate, trade policy, foreign direct investment, privatization, deregulation, and property rights. Specific guidelines for developing countries on these 10 policy areas were identified as the Washington Consensus by Williamson (1990). It is beyond the scope of this book to provide comprehensive coverage but two economic strategies will be discussed.

Import-Substitution

If an import-substitution strategy is followed, then a country tries to replace foreign imports with domestic production. This strategy tries to protect domestic industries, increases self-reliance, and can reduce the amount of money paid to other countries. In order to encourage import substitution, a government can use policies such as subsidizing domestic companies, forms of taxation, protectionist trade policies, and can go as far as nationalizing foreign companies. In the twentieth century, import substitution was used by many countries in Latin America but also by, for example, Romania which, in the 1970s and 1980s under President Ceausescu, invested heavily to develop its own industries. Another example is Spain, which, in the 1940s and later under President Franco, tried to become self-sufficient. International businesses can play an important role in this economic strategy because these companies may sell raw materials or provide technologies that a country needs.

In practice import substitution has often not been successful due to its underlying assumptions. This type of economic strategy has limited applicability for smaller countries due to a limited home market or countries with consumers that have limited income levels because they have limited ability to purchase domestically produced goods. Another drawback is that it provides little incentive for domestic companies to reduce costs or improve products. Import substitution has often resulted in high government spending with consequences such as inflation, debt, and so forth. A policy that governments have used to limit their spending is to engage in offset or countertrade arrangements. Countertrade ties an import to an export (Marin and Schnitzer 1995). Offset arrangements mean that in order for a multinational company to sell specific products in a country, it is required to produce something in that country. For example, when Romania purchased BAC 1–11 aircraft in 1968 from the British Aircraft Corporation it was able to reach an agreement with the UK for the licensed production of the Britten-Norman islander. This illustrates the sometimes complicated political situation when doing international business because although aircraft were bought from one UK-based company, production was moved to Romania by another, unrelated, UK-based company. Countertrade means that payment is not made with money but instead with goods, for example, agricultural products.

Export-Oriented

If an export-oriented strategy is followed, then a country utilizes its advantages to export products in world markets. There are essentially two types of advantages, that is, absolute advantages and comparative advantages. Although it is beyond the scope of this book to have an in-depth discussion on trade theories, since the distinction is often misunderstood and the term comparative advantage is frequently used when an absolute advantage is identified, both will be briefly explained.

A country has a competitive or absolute advantage if it can produce certain goods cheaper than other countries. Assume a simple situation with two countries, Country X and Country Y. Both countries have 200 resources and the resource cost for production is shown in Table 3.2. Before trade, both countries use half their resources for the production of Product A and half of their resources for the production of Product B.

In this situation, Country X has an absolute advantage in product A, that is, it is cheaper for Country X compared to Country Y to produce Product A. Country Y has an absolute advantage in product B, that is, it is cheaper for Country Y compared to Country X to produce Product B. If both countries specialize in the product for which they have

Table 3.2 *Resource cost for production, absolute advantage*

Country	Resource required for 1 product A	Resource required for 1 product B	Product mix before trade
Country X	10	20	10A and 5B
Country Y	40	10	2.5A and 10B

an absolute advantage, then Country X will produce 20 Product A and Country Y will produce 20 Product B. Let us assume that they then trade six quantities of Product A for six quantities of Product B. Thus, Country X will then have 14A and 6B and Country Y will have 6A and 14B. Both countries are better off with specialization and trade!

A country has a comparative advantage when it does not have an absolute advantage, but, when considering other countries and trade, it still makes sense to specialize. Assume the same simple situation with two countries, Country X and Country Y. Both countries still have 200 resources but with slightly different resource cost for production as shown in Table 3.3. Before trade, both countries use half their resources for the production of Product A and half of their resources for the production of Product B.

In this situation, Country X has a competitive or absolute advantage in Product A, that is, it is cheaper for Country X compared to Country Y to produce Product A. Country X also has an absolute advantage in Product B, that is, it is cheaper for Country X compared to Country Y to produce Product B. In other words, Country X is better at producing both products. Nevertheless, it can still be beneficial for both countries to specialize and trade by looking at the comparative advantage. Country X has a comparative advantage in Product A because it can produce four times the quantity of Product A but *only* one-and-a-half times the quantity of Product B that Country Y can produce. Therefore, Country Y will specialize in Product B (producing 10B). Country X will produce more of Product A (producing 15A and 3.75B). Let us assume that they then trade four quantities of Product A for four quantities of Product B. Thus, Country X will then have 11A and 7.75B and Country Y will have 4A and 6B. Despite the fact that Country X is better at producing both Product A as well as Product B, it is still in the best interest for both countries to specialize based on their comparative advantage.

Table 3.3 Resource cost for production, comparative advantage

Country	Resource required for 1 product A	Resource required for 1 product B	Product mix before trade
Country X	10	13 1/3	10A and 7.5B
Country Y	40	20	2.5A and 5B

The export-oriented strategy is typically a more open strategy than the import-substitution strategy. It frequently has limited subsidies, open market access, limited trade barriers, and so forth. In the twentieth century, this strategy was particularly used by East Asian economies such as Singapore, Hong Kong, and Taiwan. International businesses can play an important role in this economic strategy. Companies can, for example, produce products or parts that are exported back to the home market while also upgrading and training the domestic workforce. One of the weaknesses of this strategy is its dependency on and thus vulnerability toward external markets.

Technological Development

Technological development is directly related to economic development. As the discussion in the previous section demonstrated, economic development is related to productivity improvements. Many productivity improvements are the result of technological developments. Therefore, governments, especially of developing countries, are frequently interested in technological upgrading. Often, this is accomplished by attracting foreign businesses that possess advanced technologies. In terms of Figure 3.1, this is a potential method to catch-up relatively quickly with more economically advanced countries.

A detailed schema for technological development was developed by Sharif (1988) and further developed by the Technology Atlas Team and its individual members (see, e.g., Bowonder and Miyake 1988; Ramanathan 1988). They view technology as consisting of four components, see the section Producing Products in Chapter 2 and Figure 2.3; Figure 3.2 provides an abbreviated view of technological development.

Figure 3.2 illustrates the connection between technology at the firm level, the industry level, the sector level, and finally what that means for the national level. Governments can use this approach to assess the different levels and to determine a strategy for improvement. International companies play an important role because they provide the technology content at the most basic level. For example, back in the 1970s when Ford invested in South Africa it spent considerable resources in training hundreds of local employees for months on end (Behrman and Wallender 1976). The role of foreign multinational companies has, for instance, been

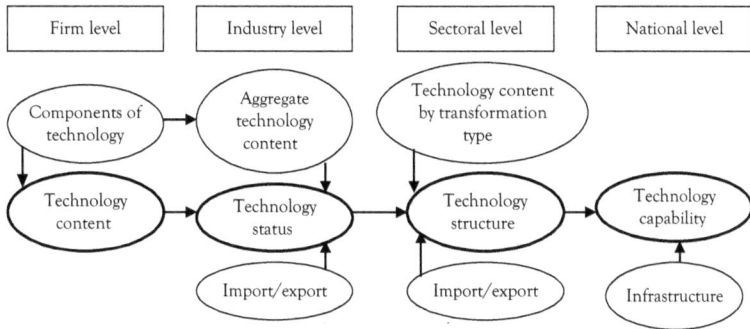

Figure 3.2 Technological development

Source: Adapted from Sharif (1988).

considered crucial for the development of Korea's electronics industry while the government's role was limited (Cyhn 2002). For companies this may provide insight as to why a government is trying to attract them, what type of technology governments are looking for, and might provide insight into the cost for aiding the technological development process.

Technology Development Strategies

Technological upgrading is a very challenging task. As mentioned earlier, when considering Figure 3.1, countries that are at low levels of development can have much higher growth rates than the upper boundary growth rate. This is because they can learn from other countries.

Often, the sequence of technological upgrading has followed the following pattern: importing sophisticated products, licensed production, joint development, indigenous development, and production. In other words, it starts at the bottom and slowly upgrades the types of activities that a country gets engaged in. In commercial aircraft production, Indonesia and China provide examples of this technological development strategy. In 1976, Indonesia started the licensed production of the C-212 from CASA in Spain. This was followed in 1979 with the joint development with CASA of the CN235. Indonesia then embarked on developing and designing its own indigenous aircraft, the N250 and the N2130. It was not able to complete this last phase for these two aircraft due to the Asia crisis. China followed a similar pattern. In the 1980s, it started the licensed production based on kits of the MD-82 from

McDonnell-Douglas in the United States. This was followed in 2002 with the development of the ARJ21 for which western parties were used to consult. The latest aircraft is the C919 that is currently in development.

This pattern of starting at the bottom and slowly upgrading may seem logical but the results from Indonesia and China indicate that it is not easy. There is also an issue with the underlying assumptions. For example, knowing how to produce some aircraft parts does not mean understanding the design of the parts. In commercial aircraft production, Brazil provides an example of a top-down approach. That means starting with R&D and following this with production while over time getting involved in more complicated products. In 1965, Brazil started to design a small aircraft, the EMB-110. It then used this design as a basis and in 1985 developed it into the EMB-120. In 1989, it then developed this further into the ERJ 135/140/145 family of jet aircraft. In 1999, it started a fresh design of the ERJ 170/175/190/195 family. Brazil has a well-developed aviation industry so this approach might be a better approach to follow. It is also more logical that when one knows how to design a product, one also has ideas on how to produce it. Figure 3.3 illustrates the two approaches.

Whatever technological upgrading strategy a country follows, there is a crucial role for international companies because international companies offer access to advanced and productive technologies. For a country

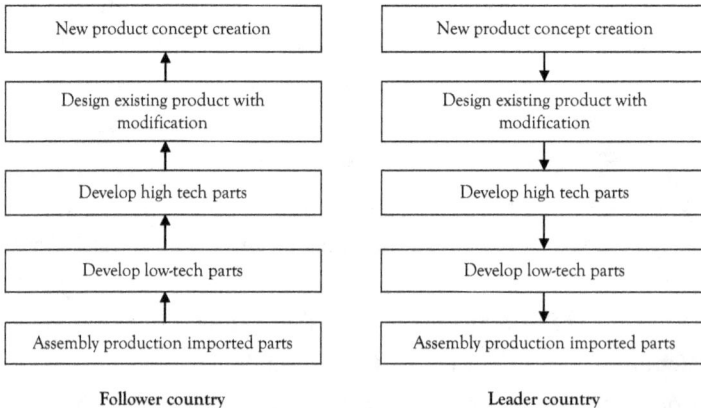

Figure 3.3 Development path

Source: Adapted from Lee and Lim (2001).

that has an overall low level of technological sophistication, it might be beneficial to attract relatively simple production technologies. For example, in 1996 Costa Rica attracted Intel to set up an assembly and testing plant in Belén, with an initial investment of $125 million. Costa Rica was interested in attracting Intel because the Intel investment was offering a large amount of foreign direct investment. It consisted of higher value-added activities and more high-technology production than were typical for Costa Rica at that time. In combination with this, Costa Rica improved its education system leading to better qualified workers, that is, more productive, who then had the potential of working in the Intel plant for improved salaries. Intel was looking for another assembly test site because at that time most of this was done in Malaysia and the Philippines. In order to spread risk (Malaysia and the Philippines were at that time not all that stable), Intel was interested in setting up a plant in another location in the world. South America was attractive because Intel was expecting to conduct more business in South America in the future and South America was closer to the United States than, for example, South Africa.

Countries, especially when they have large domestic markets, often have the ability to force companies to share their technologies. For example, in 1974 Brazil represented the largest single export market for U.S. light aircraft manufacturers. When it decided to develop its domestic industry, Brazil sent a mission to the three major U.S. small manufacturers (Piper, Beech, and Cessna) to solicit proposals on a production agreement. Each was told that for a limited time the U.S. manufacturer would have a monopoly but during that time period Embraer desired to develop their capabilities. Once the technology was acquired, the Brazilian market would be exclusively for Embraer. Similarly, for companies that wanted to do business in China, joint ventures were typically required.

Challenges

From the perspective of a developing country, technological catch up or leapfrogging is easier said than done. Leapfrogging is when a technology generation is skipped. For example, from moving to having no telecommunication abilities to the use of cell phones and skipping the technology generation of landline phones. One of the variables that influences the relative ease of learning, that is, catching-up, is the absorptive capacity. The absorptive capacity is defined as the ability of a firm to recognize the value of new, external information, assimilate it, and apply it to commercial ends (Cohen and Levinthal 1990). This is largely a function of the firm's level of prior related knowledge but also relates to the previously discussed concept of integrated industry, that is, how dependent is it upon the environment. The concept of absorptive capacity is essentially about whether it is possible to learn about the new technology and whether it can be comprehended, and if so, how challenging that would be. The key question is whether things are *in place* that allow the absorption. To use a metaphor, it would be extremely challenging to teach second grade students how to do calculus. This is because the second grade students do not have the right background that would allow them to understand calculus. In a very optimistic viewpoint, it might be possible to teach them a few calculus tricks that may give the impression that they can do calculus. However, they would lack the general comprehension. To build up the general level of comprehension that would allow them to understand calculus would probably take years. The same applies when introducing sophisticated technologies into environments that are not developed far enough, that is, the absorptive capacity is too low. Evidence of this can be seen when governments force an international company to localize certain activities. Figure 3.4 illustrates the experiences of the American

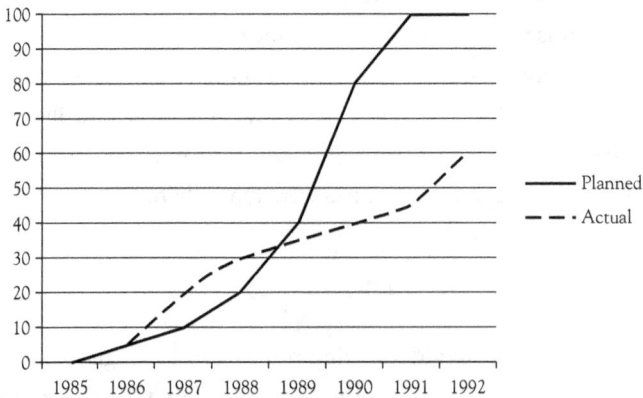

Figure 3.4 *Localization process of Beijing Jeep*

Source: Based on Jia (1993).

Motor Corporation in China. It had to follow a path with increasing local content but as the graph shows, it was not able to do so, for example, due to a lack of an adequate local infrastructure and reliable supplies.

Related to this, despite the ability of governments to *force* companies to move manufacturing to their country through, for example, joint venture requirements, they do not always gain the technologies that they are trying to attract. This is because companies are essentially using the same concept of absorptive capacity and often only transfer technologies that a country is able to absorb. That means, for example, transferring manufacturing tasks for which skills already exist or that take relatively little additional training because transferring more complicated tasks adds additional risk. In other words, the receiving country does not benefit that much.

Even if the country is able to attract more sophisticated technologies, it is not trivial that this has a positive effect on the country. Although on the one hand technology can lead to productivity improvements that can lead to improved economic performance, on the other hand, productivity improvements may also lead to job losses.

From an advanced country's perspective, there are concerns when other countries are attracting companies to relocate their operations, that is, to engage in offshore production (Jahns, Hartmann, and Bals 2006). Offshoring is ill-defined but typically means that production is taking place in a country not in close proximity and can be internal to the company, external (buy), or a mix (joint venture). One concern is hollowing-out. Hollowness is defined as the percentage of domestic firms' total domestic sales originating from their foreign affiliates (Kotabe 1989). Another, related concern is the degrading of the industrial commons. The industrial commons are the collective capabilities that serve its industry, including suppliers of advanced materials, tools, production equipment, and components (Pisano and Shih 2009). For example, due to offshore production and outsourcing that has taken place in the past, the industrial commons in the United States have been diminished in several areas. The United States can no longer produce a range of products including but not limited to fabless chips, compact fluorescent lighting, and advanced composites used in sporting goods and other consumer gear (Pisano and Shih 2009).

From a company perspective, another risk is related to intellectual property protection. One of the companies that learned this lesson is General Motors. In 2004, General Motors Daewoo filed a lawsuit against Chery, a Chinese manufacturer. General Motors claimed that the Chery mini-car QQ was a copy of its Daewoo Matiz and that many parts were interchangeable. The lawsuit was settled in 2005 out of court. While visiting Bangkok, Thailand, in 2008 I came across another example. In one of the streets there was a row of tables with jewelry and watches. As an aviation enthusiast I was aware of the expensive Breitling watches but did not see many on the tables. A simple inquiry showed it was not a problem. The sellers had catalogues of products and although not on display they did have Breitling watches. A near-perfect replica of a Breitling Navitimer watch could be bought for about $25 while in the United States these watches sell for $5,000 or more. Obviously this is not good news for Breitling. Similar approaches to sales can also be found elsewhere such as in Porto Alegre (Brazil) where sellers of shoes and cell phones walk the streets with catalogues with pictures. Countries differ in terms of law enforcement of intellectual property. This also relates to law enforcement against the import of illegal products. For example, many Dutch tourists upon return from a trip to Turkey are pulled aside at the Schiphol airport and fake brand name clothing is confiscated and people are fined. In airports in the United States there is less enforcement.

Another issue for companies to consider is changing conditions, especially after initial incentives to relocate have expired. A company that experienced this was Flextronics. In early 2000, Flextronics invested in a plant in Brno. The Czech Republic provided Flextronics with $3.5 million in subsidies for creating new jobs and income tax relief. Seven hectares of land were transferred to Flextronics for a symbolic amount (less than one dollar) and no rent was charged for an additional 38 hectares. Flextronics committed to invest at least $10 million in three years on technology, equipment, and training people. By mid-May, Flextronics announced that it would transfer production to China. The worldwide changing industrial conditions meant that Flextronics had to reduce its capacity. Reduction in the Czech Republic was further driven by appreciation currency and rising labor cost, for more information see Štrach and Everett (2007).

Implications for Managing International Operations

This chapter has discussed the role of the government and how governments, for a variety of reasons, may be interested in attracting businesses. The main point to take away is that although on the one hand governments can impose regulations on companies, on the other hand companies have bargaining power related to the motives that governments have. It is important for international operations managers to recognize the context in which they operate. To gain insight and sensitivity to the government's underlying motives, a manager can do the following:

- First, it is important to understand the characteristics of different levels of economic development and how the level of economic development influences how governments approach businesses. This chapter has provided some basics in this regard. For additional insight, Porter (1990) and Porter, Ketels, and Delgado (2007) are recommended. Following this, the manager needs to determine the type of economy at the domestic location, that is, factor-driven, investment-driven, or innovation-driven stage. A good resource for this is the Global Competitiveness Report, which is available online by the World Economic Forum (www.weforum.org). This provides insight into the advantages and disadvantages of the environmental context in which the company operates.

- Next, the manager needs to determine what type of economy the country that is considered for operations represents, how this is different from the domestic location, and what the implications are from an operations management perspective for operating in a potentially different type of economy. For example, if the domestic country is an innovation-driven economy whereas the international location under consideration is a factor-driven economy, then there are differences in level of infrastructure, technology, laws, and regulations. More on this will be provided in Chapter 4. Another important aspect that needs to be assessed is whether the company is operating in an island industry or an integrated industry because an island industry is less dependent upon other existing industries.

- An additional analysis at this point is the determination of the attractiveness for the company's operations to the government. This is connected to the type of economy. For example, for a factor-driven economy, the main attraction might be the (low-level) jobs and accompanying training for employees that the company will be providing for the region. An assessment should be made of how the attractiveness of the company is connected to the weaknesses of the economy and how these weaknesses affect the productivity of the operations. For instance, if a government is interested in attracting companies that provide (low-level) jobs and training, then this might be an indication of a poorly educated or trained workforce. The government is interested in the company so that its nation's workforce is upgraded but the company should realize that this training not only costs money but in addition initial productivity may be lower due to the lower-skilled workforce.

- Then, the bargaining position of the government should be assessed. This is influenced by the domestic government and includes for instance the ability to impose countertrade. Political risks, such as for nationalization, and political requirements, such as localization of production, should also be assessed.

- Lastly, the bargaining position of the company should be assessed. This is for instance based on what it has to offer and alternatives that are available to the government.

Estimating the importance of the operations to a foreign government is necessary and important because it provides insight into the relative bargaining position. This can, for example, influence the price of land, availability of subsidies, or other operations aspects. In Chapter 4, a complementary company perspective will be provided.

Conclusion

In this chapter, a country or government perspective was taken to look at the strategies that are followed for economic and technological development. Different stages in economic development were discussed. Governments have a crucial role in economic and technological development, particularly for the early stages of development. Multinational companies play an important role for countries because they offer, among other things, employment and technologies. Depending upon its stage of development certain types of technologies or companies are more or less attractive for a country. Other concerns for governments should be whether the industry has a high dependency on other industries or not (integrated versus island), whether it has specific dependencies on location (footloose), and whether there are some common elements needed for many industries (industrial commons). These types of factors can make it more or less challenging to develop local industries.

CHAPTER 4

Advantages of Location

Toward the end of 1950, the governor of North Carolina launched the Research Triangle. The Research Triangle is an area bordered by the three research universities, that is, Duke University located in Durham, North Carolina State University located in Raleigh, and the University of North Carolina at Chapel Hill. One of the objectives was to create a place that would attract research-oriented companies. An advantage of the location was that the region offered a highly educated local work force and was in close proximity to the state's research universities. Although progress was slow for 20 years, in the last couple of decades significant progress has been made. For example, in 2001, I visited the Kenan Institute on North Carolina State University's Centennial Campus and noticed the difference with regular universities. The Centennial Campus was established by the end of the 1980s and provides an environment where businesses and university departments are mixed together. University–industry collaboration is enhanced because companies are literally located in the same building as university researchers. It is therefore no surprise that there are, and have been, many industry–university collaborative research centers in that geographic location. Benefits of this colocation and cooperation include knowledge spillovers, that is, synergy, and lower cost of doing business, that is, improved productivity. Another example is Silicon Valley for high-technology businesses, in particular related to computer chips. Despite the higher number of competitors, this type of location is attractive because it offers among other things skilled employees, opportunities for collaboration, technology transfer with universities, and the availability of venture capital for start-up companies.

The reasons why governments try to attract businesses to their country were discussed in Chapter 3. The purpose of this chapter is to delve deeper into what locations have to offer for businesses. Section

Output Conditions will focus on the output side of things while section *Input Conditions* will focus on the input side of things.

Output Conditions

At the end of the production line is the customer, that is, the output goes to the customer. Many companies are therefore attracted to locations that offer markets for their products. Thus, BRIC countries (Brazil, Russia, India, and China) are attractive because they offer large populations. With improving economic conditions, the consumers in these countries have more money available for purchasing products. For instance, China's population is estimated at around 1.3 billion and the average income level measured by gross domestic product (GDP) per capita (purchase power parity or PPP) is estimated at $9,055 making China a huge potential market.

However, a deeper analysis is necessary to determine a more accurate market size. Having average indicators such as GDP per capita is not sufficient because the average may have limited meaning. Compare the following two situations. In situation A, there are 100 people each earning exactly $10,000. In this situation, the mean income level is $10,000. In situation B, there are 10 people who earn $82,000 each and 90 people who earn $2,000 each. The market potential for these two situations, despite the same average, is quite different. Instead of looking at the average income, it is more meaningful to look at income distributions. The GINI coefficient for income distribution is a helpful tool to look at income distribution. The GINI coefficient for income distribution measures the inequality among levels of income. A value of zero for the GINI coefficient represents perfect equality (as described in situation A earlier). A value of one represents maximal inequality. Figure 4.1 shows, for selected countries, the GINI coefficient.*

Another way of looking at this is to look at the percentage share of the total income by groups in the population.

---

* Besides the World Bank, information is also available from other sources. See, e.g., http://www.gfmag.com/tools/global-database/economic-data/11944-wealth-distribution-income-inequality.html#axzz2v2PwSQiL

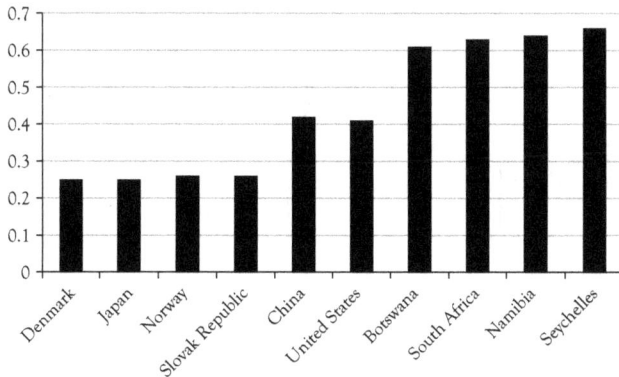

Figure 4.1 Lowest and highest GINI coefficient for income distribution
Source: Based on World Bank data.

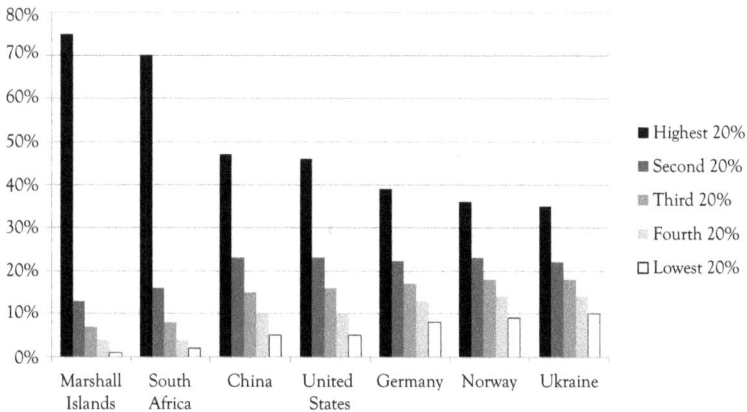

Figure 4.2 Income distribution by population segments
Source: Based on World Bank data.

Figure 4.2 provides an example where the population is divided in five segments of the population and illustrates each segment's share of the total income. This type of analysis provides a much better sense about the potential market size than looking at average income levels for a country as a whole.

Insight into the distribution of age groups across the entire population is another important factor for determining market potential. In this regard, population pyramids are useful because they show population size by age bracket. Examples of population pyramids are provided in Figure 4.3, which is based on United Nations data.*

---

* See: http://esa.un.org/wpp/

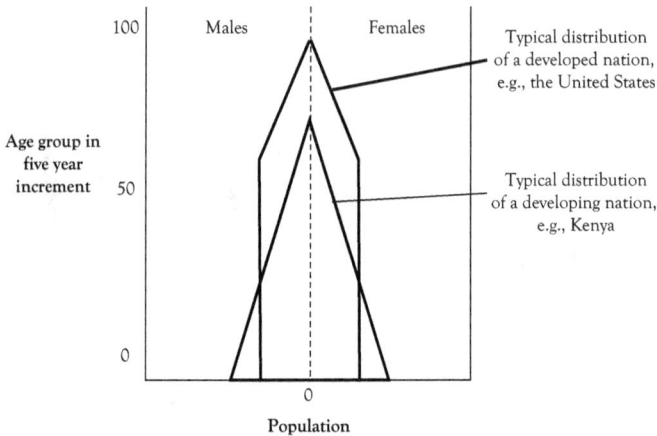

Figure 4.3 Population pyramid examples

The pattern that is commonly found for developing countries is the pyramid shape, that is, wide at the bottom and narrow at the top. Advanced nations have a pattern that has more similarities with a rectangular shape in the bottom. Population and income distributions are helpful for determining what markets a country has to offer.

As discussed in Chapter 2 with several examples, cultural characteristics play a crucial role for the overall size of the market. For example, Dalgic and Heijblom (1996) describe the strategic alliance experience of a European building company with two Malaysian partners. Demand for their houses was discouraging and they found out that the material used, that is, reinforced concrete that was common in Europe, was a primary reason because it did not fit well with the local culture. The challenge with these types of cultural issues is that with hindsight they are often easy to explain but they can be difficult to predict in advance. Many companies have underestimated this aspect, do not do sufficient market research, or do not use people who are knowledgeable in this regard. The result can be an overly optimistic view of the international market potential.

Overall, in order to get a good sense for the potential market size it is crucial to look at income and population distribution, as well as to determine the influence of culture on the demand for the product and its particular characteristics.

Input Conditions

Countries also offer inputs to companies, mainly the workforce and raw materials. For example, Axiom, a U.S. manufacturer of fishing rods set up a plant in Mexico to take advantage of low labor cost. Another example is that in recent years several Chinese (mining) companies, such as the China National Nuclear Corporation, have invested in Africa due to the availability of minerals. Nevertheless, locating close to raw materials does not always have the desired result as Celanese discovered when it purchased land to open a plant in Sicily to take advantage of local trees as raw material. There were not enough trees and they were too small. Celanese ended up importing them from Canada instead (Ricks 1995). There are also situations where companies take advantage of less strict (environment) regulation when locating internationally. Although at face value a lack of environmental restrictions might have some advantages, it can also come at a high cost. For example, while visiting a scooter factory in Malaysia in 2009 it was noticeable that at the end of the assembly line where the product was tested, there were no systems to deal with exhaust fumes. They were simply going into the factory, which is rather unhealthy. A more severe example comes from Pakistan where in September 2012 almost 300 textile workers died in a factory fire in Karachi. Also, in November 2012 over 110 textile workers died in a factory fire in Dhaka, Bangladesh. These factories had limited enforcement of regulations with regard to fire safety.

The promise of better input conditions in other countries often makes them attractive. Similar to the output conditions, a careful analysis is required to determine whether input conditions are indeed overall better.

The World Economic Forum (WEF) annually publishes the Global Competitiveness Report (GCR), which contains a ranking of countries, that is, the global competitiveness index, and is a helpful tool for more sophisticated analysis of the input conditions. The competitiveness of a country "is defined as the set of institutions, policies, and factors that determine the level of productivity of a country. The level of productivity, in turn, sets the level of prosperity that can be reached by an economy. The productivity level also determines the rates of return obtained by

Table 4.1 Competitiveness of countries

	First	Second	Third	Fourth	Fifth
2000	U.S.	Singapore	Luxembourg	Netherlands	Ireland
2001	Finland	U.S.	Canada	Singapore	Australia
2002	U.S.	Finland	Taiwan	Singapore	Sweden
2003	Finland	U.S.	Sweden	Denmark	Taiwan
2004	Finland	U.S.	Sweden	Taiwan	Denmark
2005	Finland	U.S.	Sweden	Denmark	Taiwan
2006	Switzerland	Finland	Sweden	Denmark	Singapore
2007	U.S.	Switzerland	Denmark	Sweden	Germany
2008	U.S.	Switzerland	Denmark	Sweden	Singapore
2009	Switzerland	U.S.	Singapore	Sweden	Denmark
2010	Switzerland	Sweden	Singapore	U.S.	Germany
2011	Switzerland	Singapore	Sweden	Finland	U.S.
2012	Switzerland	Singapore	Finland	Sweden	Netherlands
2013	Switzerland	Singapore	Finland	Germany	U.S.
2014	Switzerland	Singapore	U.S.	Finland	Germany

Source: Based on World Economic Forum.

investments in an economy, which in turn are the fundamental drivers of its growth rates" (Schwab and Sala-I Martin 2013).

Table 4.1 provides an overview of the top five countries in the global competitiveness index since 2000. This illustrates that in particular Singapore, the United States, and north European countries have consistently ranked high. This is a reflection of their high level of productivity, and through this these nations have achieved high levels of prosperity for its citizens.

Since the global competitiveness index is a reflection of the productivity of a country, it is helpful for companies to examine the index when considering to set up in another country. Similar to Porter (1990) (see Chapter 3), the WEF classifies countries into stages of development. The WEF recognizes five stages based on GDP per capita. This is illustrated in Table 4.2. The difference between GNI and GDP is that GNI is the total value of goods and services produced within a country (i.e., GDP) plus income received from other countries (such as interest and dividends) minus similar payments made to other countries.

The WEF classification is helpful because it provides insight into the overall level of productivity of a country and its barriers to improving

Table 4.2 *Stages of development*

Stage of development	GDP per capita in 2012	Example country
Factor-driven economy	< $2,000	India and Vietnam
Transition from stage 1 to stage 2	≥$2,000 but <$3,000	Bolivia and Libya
Efficiency-driven economy	≥$3,000 but <$9,000	China and South Africa
Transition from stage 2 to stage 3	≥$9,000 but ≤$17,000	Brazil and Mexico
Innovation-driven economy	> $17,000	U.S. and UK

Source: Adapted from Schwab and Sala-i-Martín (2013).

the productivity, see also the discussion in the section *Economic Strategies* in Chapter 3. Labor productivity varies across the regions of the world (van de Ven and van Laarhoven 1997). Often these types of measures are based on aggregate data (see Sauian 2002; Shurchuluu 2002), and frequently cost structure differences, that is, levels of automation, are considered an explanation. However, it has also been shown that labor productivity between advanced and developing nations differ at the shop floor level. When comparing 30 plants from one multinational company and located across a dozen countries, Mefford (1986) found that management and worker-related factors were the most important determinants of labor productivity differences. It is important for companies that are looking for low labor-cost to realize that in some instances, despite much lower labor wages at the country level, the cost of production increased. This phenomenon is persistent and has been experienced for many years. Examples are Cummins engines that cost about 4.1 times more to produce in India compared to the United States (Baranson 1967, 83), a metal part fabrication that cost between 1.6 and 1.8 times more to produce in Indonesia compared to the Netherlands (van Hasselt, de Bruijn, and Wirjomartono 1977), iron from Singapore that cost 1.12 times as much as from the United States (Flaherty 1989), MD90 aircraft that cost approximately $10 million more to produce in China compared to the United States (U.S. International Trade Commission, 1998, 5–12), and passenger cars that cost between 1.2 and 1.3 times more to produce in China compared to the United States (Mackintosch and McGregor 2003). Wages play a role, but as shown in the section *Economic Strategies* in Chapter 3, as economies develop, these tend to go up. Furthermore, it is important to gain insight into what determines overall productivity, not just wages.

The countries that are ranked highest in the GCR in terms of competitiveness are able to reach high levels of productivity because they have essentially all of the *elements* in place. These *elements* in the global competitiveness index are measured through 12 groups of variables that are identified as pillars. These 12 pillars are related to the stage of development (see Figure 4.4).

Figure 4.4 illustrates that for factor-driven economies, that is, relying on basic factors of production such as an inexpensive labor pool and natural resources, the basic pillars need to be developed, that is, the institutions, infrastructure, macro environment, and health and primary education. In other words, what prohibits these countries from reaching higher levels of productivity is that they have weaknesses in one or more of these areas. A company that is considering to locate in a factor-driven stage country should be aware of these weaknesses because these weaknesses will also impact the productivity of a company. For example, toward the end of the 1990s a road trip from Mumbai to Pune in India, a distance of about 140 miles, took over 6 hours because the infrastructure (roads) was poorly developed. Obviously, spending a high amount of time on the road is not very efficient. Similarly, working in very hot conditions in India because the air condition is not available or is not working due to power outages or the opposite, that is, working in cold conditions in Romania because the heat is not working, has a negative effect on worker productivity. This type of infrastructure affects worker productivity because, for example, typing while your hands feel frozen goes a lot slower than under normal

Factor-driven	Efficiency-driven	Innovation-driven
Institutions	Higher education and training	Business sophistication
Infrastructure	Goods market efficiency	Innovation
Macro environment	Labor market efficiency	
Health and primary education	Financial market development	
	Technological readiness	
	Market size	

Figure 4.4 Drivers by stage of development

Source: Adapted from Schwab and Sala-i-Martín (2013).

working conditions. A company can, for example, install a generator but this is an additional cost that has to be incorporated in the plans. Another example from India was when in 1995 I was witnessing how they were building a hotel next to where I was staying. Much of the work was done with relatively low labor productivity due to the *technology* that was being used. For instance, women typically carried bowls with bricks on their heads up the stairs for constructing walls. Compare this with the tools and machines used in countries such as the United States, which help people to be more productive. At some point, a wall was constructed but within a few feet, there was a palm tree. In some instances, the palm tree is actually left in place and might even be part of the house, that is, the house is built around it. In this case, it was decided to remove the tree. Hence, some people went to the third floor of the hotel under construction and by using large *knives* started to cut into the tree. Needless to say, it took a long time before it was cut. Then, the process had to be repeated a floor lower. Eventually, after almost a day's work, the tree was cut. Compare this with the use of a chainsaw that would have taken only a couple of minutes. Sometimes this is a matter of finances but sometimes advanced machines are not locally available. A company can decide to ship them over but this leads to additional cost. In stark contrast to experiences in India is Sweden. During the winter months, portions of highways are heated so that there is no snow on the road. In other words even during winter months, traffic was not much affected. This is an example of how a country provides an environment that allows its citizens to have a high productivity level. A similar example was mentioned in Chapter 2 where I discussed the personal scanner that can be used for supermarket shopping, which saves time and thus improves productivity. It is therefore no surprise that Sweden is consistently ranked very high on the global competitiveness index (see Table 4.1), while India, although in the meantime the roads have improved, is still considered to be in the factor-driven stage.

The GCR provides a score for each country for each of the pillars and in addition for many underlying variables. This information provides companies with the opportunity to assess overall levels of productivity, the barriers to reaching higher levels of productivity, and how it compares with the home country. Thus, it allows for an estimate of the total cost of operating in a different country that goes well beyond looking only at labor cost per hour. The index for each pillar is based on multiple subindexes. For instance, the institutions pillar is based on measures for 21 underlying subindexes. These are property rights, intellectual property protection, diversion of public funds, public trust in politicians, irregular payments and bribes, judicial independence, favoritism in decisions of government officials, wastefulness of government spending, burden of government regulation, efficiency of legal frameworks and settling disputes, efficiency of legal framework in challenging regulations, transparency of government policy making, business cost of terrorism, business cost of crime and violence, organized crime, reliability of police services, ethical behavior of firms, strength of auditing and reporting standards, efficacy of corporate boards, protection of minority shareholders' interests, and strength of investor protection. Each of these underlying subindexes can be a cause for low efficiency. For instance, in Romania in 1998 there was a fairly high level of corruption.* This was noticeable when parts had to come from overseas and would not be delivered on time because they got *stuck* at customs, that is, could not be found. With additional payment they could be found. This means that corruption has a negative effect on efficiency because it either takes longer or because it costs more money to get goods into the country.

Corruption is typically a reality when operating internationally. Corruption affects overall costs, image, and as a result overall productivity. Corruption can take many forms, most commonly in bribery, embezzlement and fraud, extortion, blackmail, abuse of discretion, nepotism, or exploiting conflicts of interest. Generally, it is recognized that there may be both legal and illegal forms of corruption. Legal corruption involves processes that are technically legal in a country but that still result in private or personal gain by a few key players (Kaufmann and Vicente 2011). For example, the use of favors or personal connections may not specifically violate a country's laws but would still be considered corrupt on moral and economic grounds (Dalton 2005). It may appear that in many

---

* Apart from the GCR, another source for insight into corruption is Transparency International. They developed the corruption perception index—see: www. transparency.org.

instances it might be virtually impossible to operate without bribing, but recent examples illustrate the costs when it is pursued in court. In April 2013, Philips settled a bribery case in Poland for $4.5 million; in late 2013, former Siemens executives were charged in a case involving more than $100 million in bribes in Argentina; in April 2014, GlaxoSmithKline was accused of bribing doctors in Poland while already involved in other cases in China and Iraq; and in April 2014, Hewlett Packard agreed to pay $108 million for bribing in Poland, Russia, and Mexico.

Efficiency-driven and innovation-driven countries typically offer higher productivity but have higher wages as well. One of the appeals of these countries is that in these countries competitive clusters start to develop. Initially these clusters are shallow, but clusters can also be vertically very deep, for example, with world competitive related and supplier industries, or horizontally wide, that is, covering a range of industries. The clustering of economic activities and employment may happen because of characteristics of the region. For example, Pullman, Washington (United States), and Greenville, North Carolina (United States), have a cluster or concentration in healthcare in terms of employments. The reason for this is that these are relatively isolated cities and thus serve as a healthcare destination for surrounding areas. The clustering of economic activities and employment can also happen because the region is more internationally competitive as shown through exports. Examples of these types of competitive clusters are the watch industry in Switzerland, the flower industry in the Netherlands, and the aircraft industry in the Seattle area (United States). These clusters offer (productivity) advantages for firms due to advanced workforce skills, linkages between firms, with suppliers, related industries, institutes, knowledge spillover, and so forth. For instance, a company interested in growing cut flowers would be well-advised to be involved in the Dutch flower cluster. That is, because aside from the Dutch flower auction system, which plays a prominent role in worldwide cut-flower trade, the inputs available in the Netherlands are amongst the most advanced in the world. There is, among others, expertise in growing bulbs, in building greenhouses, in soil treatments, in climate control and accelerating cut-flower crops, in advanced harvesting machines, and in developing new cut-flower varieties. Therefore, the geographic location of a competitive cluster can be appealing for companies not because of low factor cost such as cheap labor, but instead because it offers knowledge and expertise that enhances productivity.

In addition to analyzing the stage of development of a country and related to this in more detail the business environment to assess the overall effect on productivity, another issue to consider is the level of automation. When a company is planning on moving production from a high-labor cost country to a low-labor cost country to take advantage of the lower wages, it needs to determine the actual labor content in the production process. Only high labor content processes would benefit from this move. High labor content processes typically have lower labor productivity. For example, in 1995 at an electronic transformer manufacturing company in Bangalore, India, they used labor-intensive manual processes to wind electronic transformers. The annual production with approximately 10 employees achieved in this manner in India could be accomplished in less than a week with the advanced (expensive) automated transformer winding machines that were available in Western Europe at that time. Moving the automated production from Western Europe to India in that case would not have made sense because the automated processes involved little labor, and hence little money could be saved on labor cost.

Lastly, there is the question of how connected the company, and its processes, is with its environment. This is related to the industrial commons concept discussed in Chapter 3. For example, for manufacturing processes the quality of available materials in advanced countries is often not available in developing countries because suppliers do not have the same level of sophistication. Consequently, companies might have to import the materials, which is less efficient and adds to the cost.

Estimating the Impact of the Environment on Productivity

This chapter has discussed the advantages of international locations. The main point to take away is that companies need to be careful before moving their operations to international locations. Many examples exist of companies that conducted incomplete analysis before their international investment and therefore consequently experienced disappointing results. Roughly speaking, there are two main advantages for companies in international locations, that is, domestic markets for their products and the input factors to the production process. This section will focus on the input factors to the production processes. With regard to the market potential for products, several important techniques were pointed out in this chapter to help with determining realistic markets. In addition, in Chapter 2 the cultural aspects and their influence on the purchasing process were discussed. It is recommended to involve local consultants to conduct market feasibility studies.

To gain insight and sensitivity into the influence of the overall country environment on the productivity of the production processes, a manager can do the following:

- First, the manager needs to determine the type of economy at the domestic location, that is, factor-driven, investment-driven, or innovation-driven stage. A good resource for this is the GCR, which is available online by the WEF (www.weforum.org). This provides insight into the advantages and disadvantages of the environmental context in which the company operates.
- Next, the manager needs to determine what type of economy the country that is considered for operations represents and how this is different from the domestic location.
- A follow-up to this should be an in-depth analysis of the detailed differences. A good starting point is the GCR, which provides quantitative data on over hundred variables divided into several categories, for example, higher education and training, and infrastructure. For instance, if the quality of roads, railroads, ports, and air transport is low, then this is likely to decrease the productivity because it will take more time to transport items.
- Lastly, the consequences of the detailed differences in the environments and their impact on a company's productivity in terms of cost and time should be estimated and a plan should be developed on how to deal with this impact. For instance, if the transportation infrastructure is weak, then the company can plan for this through increasing delivery lead

times to customers. Another example is that if the domestic home environment is an innovation-driven economy while the international host environment is a factor-driven economy and the motive for moving to that location is to take advantage of lower labor costs, then the production process might have to be adjusted so that more labor is involved and less automation. Changing these processes involves costs because the process planning sheets will have to be changed. Additionally, the design of the product may have to be slightly changed due to the different production processes.

Estimating the impact of operating in a different environment context on operations is necessary and important. This is particularly so because since these are environmental issues that are typically outside of the scope of the company, it is unlikely that the company can change the environment, certainly not in the short term and so this has longer-term consequences for the operations of a company

Conclusion

While Chapter 3 focused on the government or country side of things, in this chapter the orientation moved to the company side. The discussion was oriented on understanding the advantages of getting involved in international operations. With regard to the output of the production process, that is, products, one obvious motive is international markets. Many companies overestimate the size of international markets so before engaging in international sales it is important to carefully research this. Apart from cultural issues as explained in Chapter 2, other important variables to consider for estimating market size are the income levels, income distribution, and population distribution.

With regard to the production of goods, there are multiple motives for a company to move production to another country. One of the main objectives is access to low-cost production. In this chapter, it was explained that there is a relationship between the average income levels in a country and its average productivity levels. Hence, for example, low-labor-cost countries are low-labor-cost countries because certain environmental conditions form barriers to improving productivity. When considering locating in another country, companies can use information provided by the WEF to do a first level of analysis on which environmental conditions might be causing lower productivity levels and form barriers to improvement. The key lesson here is that when locating from an innovation-driven economy with high levels of productivity of the workforce to a factor-driven economy, it cannot be expected that productivity levels remain the same. The overall effect on cost, such as labor, is not trivial but is a combination of wages and labor productivity.

CHAPTER 5

Internationalization

In the middle of 2011, an interesting story came out of Georgia, United States. The story involved the *hottest* export product from the state. It caught the attention of the national media because it was a very surprising product. The company product was chopsticks and the company was called Georgia Chopsticks. Chopsticks are indeed a strange product to be producing in the United States since the local market for chopsticks is not all that large considering that most Americans eat with a knife and fork. Even stranger was that the company was set up for 100 percent export, not domestic sales. The owner of the company, originally from South Korea, set the company up to export chopsticks to China and Japan. So, why would a company in the United States be able to sell its products in China and Japan? It appeared that, for instance, Chinese companies that want to produce chopsticks have to import wood because the availability of wood in China is limited. This is due to government regulation, that is, domestic tree cutting is limited. With that one of the motives for the company was born. Instead of selling the raw material, that is, wood, to China, sell the finished, and made in the United States, final product. Unfortunately, the Georgia Chopsticks adventure did not last long as in April 2012 the company made headlines again. This time because the company was about to close. The issue was a bounced check to a supplier. The company owner publicly stated that this was simply a misunderstanding, but the company has been closed.

The purpose of this chapter is to look more closely at options that companies such as Georgia Chopsticks have available to go international. Before getting into the company side of things, the section *Trade* will explore country level descriptive trade statistics while section *Foreign Direct Investment* will explore foreign direct investment (FDI) to get a sense of what is happening worldwide. In section *Internationalization*, the path to internationalization for companies is discussed. Section

Channel for Internationalization will discuss the different types of legal entities that can be used when going international. Section *Plant Location* will discuss the decision processes for determining the international plant location while section *Outsourcing* will discuss a particular type of international operations, that is, outsourcing, in more depth. This is followed by section *Internationalization Implications and in Particular for Outsourcing* which includes recommendations for companies. Finally, some conclusions will be drawn.

Trade

International trade has expanded significantly in recent decades. Figure 5.1 shows an overview of world exports since 1990. This figure shows that from 1990 to 2012, trade has grown by over 500 percent.

Tables 5.1 and 5.2 show the largest trade countries from 2000. These tables show that much of the trade occurs from and to the United States, China, Japan, and Europe.

To provide a little more insight, the top-three countries are shown in Figures 5.2 and 5.3. These figures show the remarkable growth of China's imports and exports.

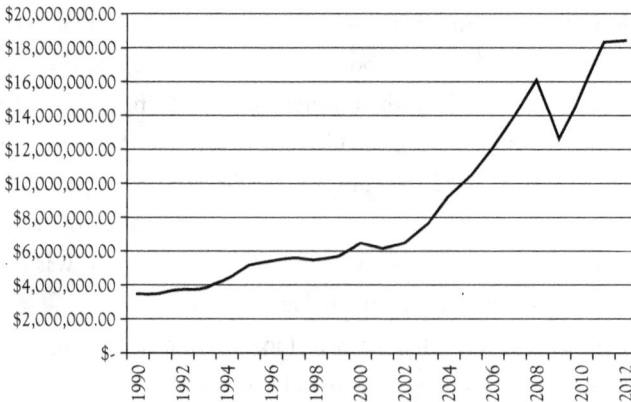

Figure 5.1 Total world export in millions of dollars*

Source: Based on World Trade Organization.

---

* Based on data provided by the World Trade Organization through their database. Available at: http://stat.wto.org

Table 5.1 Top exporting countries

	First	Second	Third	Fourth	Fifth
2000	U.S.	Germany	Japan	France	UK
2001	U.S.	Germany	Japan	France	UK
2002	U.S.	Germany	Japan	France	China
2003	Germany	U.S.	Japan	China	France
2004	Germany	U.S.	China	Japan	France
2005	Germany	U.S.	China	Japan	France
2006	Germany	U.S.	China	Japan	France
2007	Germany	China	U.S.	Japan	France
2008	Germany	China	U.S.	Japan	Netherlands
2009	China	Germany	U.S.	Japan	Netherlands
2010	China	U.S.	Germany	Japan	Netherlands
2011	China	U.S.	Germany	Japan	Netherlands
2012	China	U.S.	Germany	Japan	Netherlands

Source: Based on World Trade Organization.

Table 5.2 Top importing countries

	First	Second	Third	Fourth	Fifth
2000	U.S.	Germany	Japan	UK	France
2001	U.S.	Germany	Japan	UK	France
2002	U.S.	Germany	UK	Japan	France
2003	U.S.	Germany	China	UK	France
2004	U.S.	Germany	China	France	UK
2005	U.S.	Germany	China	UK	Japan
2006	U.S.	Germany	China	UK	Japan
2007	U.S.	Germany	China	UK	France
2008	U.S.	Germany	China	Japan	France
2009	U.S.	China	Germany	France	Japan
2010	U.S.	China	Germany	Japan	France
2011	U.S.	China	Germany	Japan	France
2012	U.S.	China	Germany	Japan	UK

Source: Based on World Trade Organization.

A really important factor when considering trade is the exchange rate. In fact, this also affects choices for FDI versus export versus licensing. The problem of course is that exchange rates are not very stable. For example, from April 1, 2013, to April 1, 2014, the lowest exchange rate was $1.28465 per euro (April 1, 2013), whereas the highest was $1.39611 per

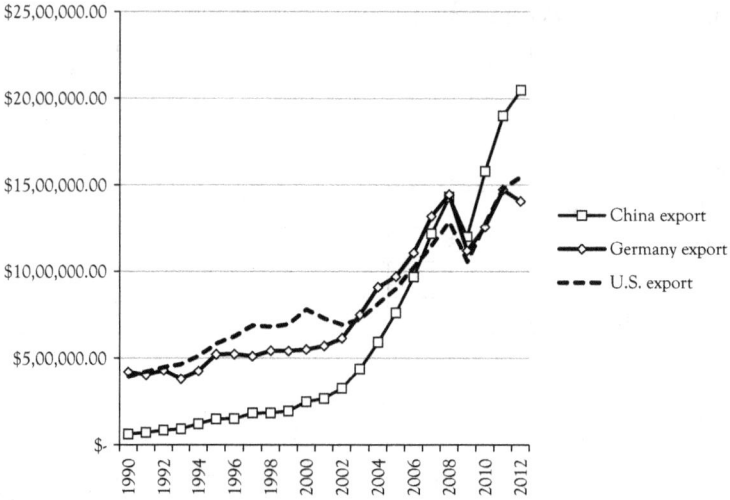

Figure 5.2 *Comparison of exports of the United States, China, and Germany (in millions of dollars)*
Source: Based on World Trade Organization.

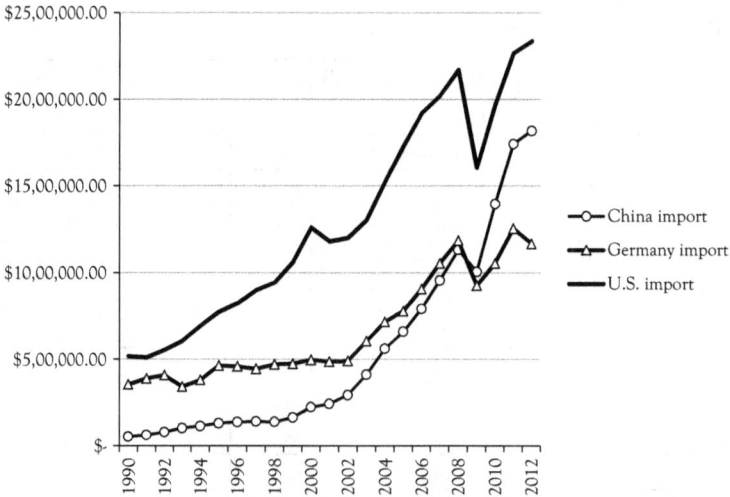

Figure 5.3 *Comparison of imports of the United States, China, and Germany (in millions of dollars)*
Source: Based on World Trade Organization.

euro (March 13, 2014). This represents more than 8.5 percent fluctuation, which considering profit margins on many products is quite substantial. Exchange rate fluctuations can easily move a profitable market into an unprofitable market and vice versa. For example, in 1996 the Dutch aircraft manufacturer Fokker filed for bankruptcy and much of this was attributed to its exchange risk exposure and the unfavorable changes in the exchange rate of the Dutch guilder (denoted by Fl.) (where production took place) versus the U.S. dollar (in which global sales occurred). This exchange rate fluctuated from Fl. 2.23 per dollar in 1987 to Fl. 1.56 per dollar in 1996, representing a change over 40 percent. One way to avoid this type of exposure is to have expenses and income in the same currency, that is, for Fokker it would have been better to have sold aircraft in Dutch currency instead of the U.S. dollar.

Note that exchange rate fluctuations always have two effects. A strengthening of a national currency will make its products more expensive for foreign markets, that is, negatively impact exports, while it will make foreign products less expensive for domestic customers, that is, positively impact imports. Vice versa, a decline in the national currency will make its products less expensive for foreign markets, that is, positively impact exports, while it will make foreign products more expensive for domestic customers, that is, a negative impact on imports. For example, the United States has in recent years argued that the Chinese Yuan Renminbi is kept at a controlled low exchange rate compared to the U.S. dollar and that if the Renminbi was allowed to freely adjust to the markets it would appraise. Currently, although the Renminbi is not pegged to the dollar, which would be a fixed exchange rate, it is only allowed to float within a narrow margin. The effect of what the United States has accused the Chinese government

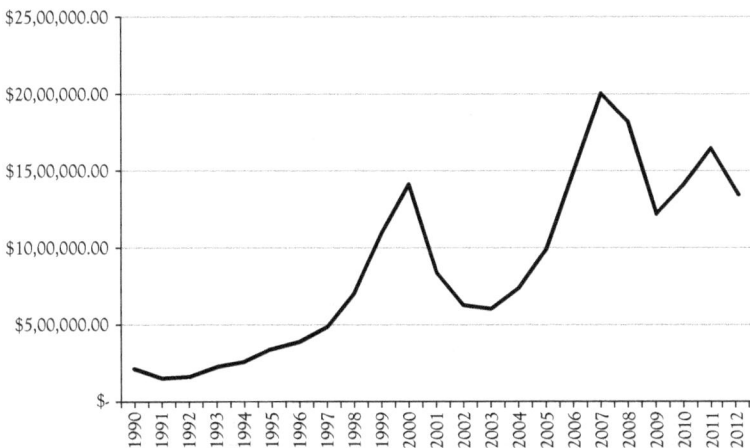

Figure 5.4 Total world FDI inflows in millions of dollars
Source: Based on United Nations (2013).

of doing is that importing from China for U.S. companies is beneficial but exporting to China for U.S. companies challenging.

Foreign Direct Investment

Similar to trade, FDI has also grown significantly in recent decades. Figure 5.4 shows an overview of foreign direct investment since 1990.

This figure shows that from 1990 to 2012, FDI has grown by over 600 percent. Tables 5.3 and 5.4 show the largest investment countries from 2000. These tables show that, similar to trade, much of the investments occur from and to the United States, China, Japan, and Europe. The FDI patterns confirm Ferdows' notion that investment in manufacturing in rich countries is not declining although the media often presents it differently:

A popular view is that manufacturing is leaving the industrialized countries and going to the developing nations. This notion is propagated every time one reads that a multinational company

Table 5.3 Top outward FDI countries

	First	Second	Third	Fourth	Fifth
2000	UK	France	U.S.	Belgium/ Luxembourg	Netherlands
2001	U.S.	Belgium/ Luxembourg	France	UK	Netherlands
2002	U.S.	UK	France	Spain	Japan
2003	U.S.	UK	Netherlands	France	Belgium
2004	U.S.	UK	Spain	France	Canada
2005	Netherlands	France	UK	Germany	Switzerland
2006	U.S.	Germany	France	Spain	UK
2007	U.S.	UK	Germany	France	Spain
2008	U.S.	Belgium	UK	France	Japan
2009	U.S.	France	Japan	Germany	Hong Kong
2010	U.S.	Germany	Hong Kong	Switzerland	China
2011	U.S.	Japan	UK	Hong Kong	Belgium
2012	U.S.	Japan	China	Hong Kong	UK

Source: Based on United Nations (2013).

Table 5.4 Top inward FDI countries

	First	Second	Third	Fourth	Fifth
2000	U.S.	Germany	UK	Belgium/ Luxembourg	Hong Kong
2001	U.S.	Belgium/ Luxembourg	UK	Netherlands	France
2002	U.S.	Germany	China	France	Spain
2003	China	U.S.	France	Belgium	Netherlands
2004	U.S.	China	UK	Belgium	Australia
2005	UK	U.S.	France	China	Germany
2006	U.S.	UK	China	France	Canada
2007	U.S.	UK	Netherlands	France	Belgium
2008	U.S.	Belgium	China	UK	Spain
2009	U.S.	China	UK	Belgium	Hong Kong
2010	U.S.	China	Belgium	Hong Kong	Germany
2011	U.S.	China	Belgium	Hong Kong	Brazil
2012	U.S.	China	Hong Kong	Brazil	British Virgin Island

Source: Based on United Nations (2013).

establishes a factory in a developing nation. These events are usually well publicized in the media. However, an investment several times larger by the same multinational company, expanding its manufacturing facilities in a highly industrialized country, often goes unnoticed by the general public. (Ferdows 1997a)

Table 5.3 shows that since 2008 Asian economies, that is, Japan, Hong Kong, and China, have become large FDI investors. Several decades ago Japan was also a large investor; it then declined but now has more FDI than before.

Table 5.4 shows that in the last couple of years, Brazil has been among the top receivers of FDI. Brazil is one of the BRIC countries (see Chapter 4). With a higher stage of development (see Table 4.2), its large population and improving economic conditions, it is not surprising that it has entered the top-tier of FDI receiving countries. This is in contrast with India which, although a large country in terms of population, is still a factor-driven economy. In 2012, India received $25.5 billion in

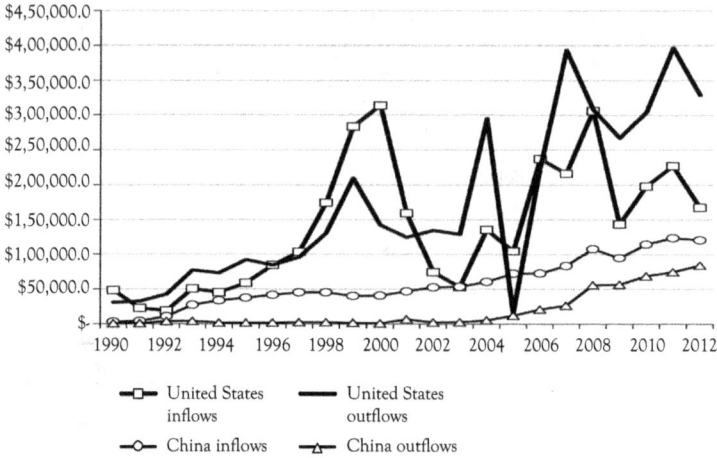

Figure 5.5 Comparison of FDI inflows and outflows of the United States and China (in millions of dollars)

Source: Based on United Nations (2013).

FDI inflows, compared to Brazil's $65.3 billion. The highest amount was received by the United States: $167.6 billion.

Since China is frequently in the news due to its economic development and large potential market, a comparison of in-flows and out-flows of FDI for the United States and China is provided in Figure 5.5. This figure illustrates that the United States still has significantly more inflows and outflows of FDI than China. In particular the outflows of China are still a bit behind.

Internationalization

There has been extensive research into how companies internationalize, what influences the path of internationalization, and the effects of international business on the countries involved. For example, there is research on the (updated) Uppsala model viewing the business environment as a network of relationships rather than the traditional approach of independent suppliers and customers. There is also research on the determinants of the mode of entry (such as exports versus FDI) including the influence of the home country. Another stream of research is concerned about the effects on the host country, for example, the job losses related to importing products rather than producing them, and yet another stream of research is concerned with how FDI leads to (or not) tech-nological upgrading, productivity improvements, and spillover effects to local companies. Here, the purpose is not to provide a detailed theoretical deliberation on these scientific developments, but rather to provide some practical insights.

The traditional theory on how companies internationalize was that companies in advanced nations would first produce and sell their prod-uct in the home market because this is where innovation takes place. In the next stage, the product would be exported to other advanced nations where there is initially limited competition because the innova-tion occurred elsewhere. When local demand is sufficient enough, for-eign factories are set up. Subsequently, export takes place to developing nations where demand starts to develop. At some point in time, the prod-uct becomes sufficiently standardized so that cost considerations start to play a major role; this is when production is shifted to developing nations (Vernon 1966). This sequence is illustrated in Figure 5.6.

This traditional model may have accurately explained how companies in the past have expanded beyond national borders but it does not reflect the situation of companies in 2014 (Camuffo et al. 2007; Khurana and Talbot 1998). Nowadays, companies are faced with different risks when operating internationally, better information availability, and changing transportation costs. In some instances, this has led to a simultaneous global launch of products. For example, in 2007 the movie *Spiderman 3* was simultaneously released in 71 countries.

It has also made it much easier than several decades ago for young companies to engage in international operations. Terms that have been used for these types of companies are international new ventures, born globals, and global start-ups. In academia, there are discussions about the exact definitions of the terms although they are often used interchangeably (Crick 2009). For example, one view is that these are companies that, from

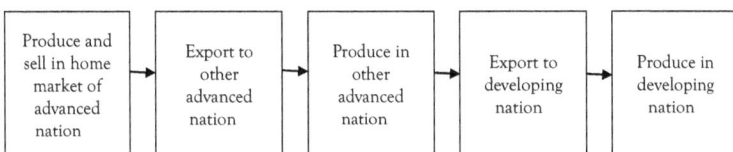

| Produce and sell in home market of advanced nation | Export to other advanced nation | Produce in other advanced nation | Export to developing nation | Produce in developing nation |

Figure 5.6 Traditional view on internationalization process

inception, seek to derive significant competitive advantage from the sale of outputs in multiple countries. Another more detailed definition is that it concerns firms that are less than 20 years old that internationalized on average within three years of founding and generated at least 25 percent of total sales from abroad (Knight, Madson, and Servais 2004). Both of these definitions relate to young companies with overseas markets. A good example is Georgia Chopsticks, mentioned earlier in the chapter, which was founded with the explicit goal of exporting its products. Apart from international markets, companies can also engage early on in international operations by locating production in other countries or purchasing parts internationally. An example is a small U.S. company that produces physical therapy products for consumers. The relatively simple products are based on wood, rope, and pulleys and can be installed on doors. The company has early on used suppliers in Asia (initially Taiwan) to supply many of the items that in some cases were still assembled and packaged for consumer use in the United States. This also provides another illustration of country differences. That is, companies in the United States are used to dealing directly with suppliers, but when dealing with Taiwanese companies it is more typical to have an intermediary. Figure 5.7 illustrates some of the different ways companies can be internationally involved.

Distinguishing the different types of international involvement is relevant because it relates to the motives of companies to get engaged internationally as well as the cost of doing so. For example, a company that produces or purchases inputs from other countries but sells in the home market has to consider the overall effectiveness and efficiency of the trade-off between producing in the home country with potentially higher production cost versus producing in a lower production cost location

		Sales	
		Domestic	International
Production	Domestic	Domestic company producing and selling in domestic market	Company that produces at home but sells in international markets
	International	A company that has international operations but sells in the home market	A company that produces and sells in many countries

Figure 5.7 International involvement

but adding in the cost of transporting the goods to the home market. This is by no means a trivial matter because the logistics involve not only the actual shipping cost but also, depending upon where it is shipped from, customs and duty fees, more expensive packaging than if shipped domestically, scrap rates for damaged goods during shipping, and possibly insurance coverage, which is another additional cost. Apart from these financial issues, there is a longer supply chain that is less agile to react to changes and there is the risk for missing parts. It is, for example, estimated that thousands of containers get lost at sea every year. Furthermore, there might be additional reputation risk due to, for example, child labor (Nike has a long history of exposure to child labor and sweatshop practices in Pakistan and Cambodia), corruption allegations (in 2012 Walmart was accused of bribes in Mexico for rezoning so that it could build its facility; Ford also experienced this in 2014 when it faced allegations that workers in China were bribing its human resource office to get a job within the company; see also section *Input Conditions* in Chapter 4), or usage of potentially dangerous chemicals (in 2007 Mattel was confronted with issues of leaded paint in China and had to recall about a million toys). Similarly, a company with sales in international markets has to consider the effectiveness and efficiency of the trade-off between producing in the home market and exporting the products and the cost involved versus setting up a plant in another country to be closer to the market.

Channel for Internationalization

One way in which a company can be involved internationally is by having a plant in another country, for example, through FDI. Investment in this manner can be both for a *greenfield plant*, that is, investing in the development and construction of a new plant, or it can be through a *brownfield plant*, that is, investment in existing facilities. FDI is by no means a trivial matter. In fact, it is in a way very surprising that a foreign company can compete against domestically raised companies that are more familiar with local tastes, laws, and so forth, and thus have several advantages compared to international companies. The OIL framework by Dunning (2000) offers much insight into why international companies are able to compete through FDI. This framework explains that in order for FDI to work there must first be ownership advantages compared to other firms of other nationalities in serving particular markets. These ownership advantages typically take the form of the possession of intangible assets. Assuming that first ownership advantages exist, second there must be internalization advantages. This means that it must be more beneficial to the firm to use them (or their output) internally themselves rather than to sell or lease them to foreign firms, for example, license. If both of these conditions exist, then third there must be locational advantages. This means that it must be in the global interests of the company to utilize these advantages in conjunction with at least some factor inputs (including natural resources) outside its home country. Otherwise foreign markets would be served by exports.

The different types of advantages give a *financial* insight into which channel a company should use when entering an international market. Another view is to look at how different channels relates to control as is illustrated in Figure 5.8.

Typically, when a company considers which channel to use, not all options are considered because not all are relevant for that company or that situation. For example, the Chinese government has forced foreign companies into joint-venture agreements by not allowing wholly owned subsidiaries.

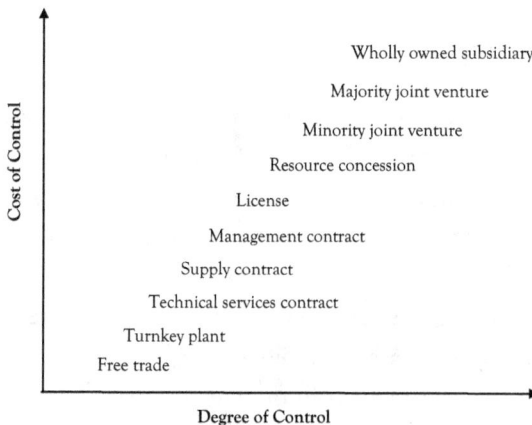

Figure 5.8 Degree and cost of control

Source: Adapted from Mason (1981).

Plant Location

When a company decides to set up a plant in a foreign country, one of the main decisions that has to be made is where to locate the plant. There is not one specific theory that answers this question. Much research has been conducted on this topic. This research shows that there are many variables influencing this process (Blair and Premus 1987), and that the variables often depend upon the situation. For manufacturing firms (Brush, Maritan, and Karnani 1999) the decision is different from that for a corporate office (Phillips 1991). For high-technology firm (Jarboe 1986), it is different from that for small companies (Mazzarol and Choo 2003). Other variables such as motive for the plant, for example, cost reduction, type of industry, and country of origin, can influence the process (Tahir and Larimo 2004; Ulgado 1996).

It is therefore not possible to present a detailed approach that will fit every firm. What can be concluded is that the site location decision generally follows a *funnel* process, see Figure 5.9. It starts broadly with the identification of a region in the world, or a little narrower, a specific country. This is followed by determining a region within a country, cities, and ultimately the plant site (Abele et al. 2008; Stevenson 2015).

At the broadest level, the most macro-oriented factors play a role, for example, the political stability, location in terms of logistics, duties, market size, and infrastructure. As the process becomes narrower, the factors that are being considered become more micro-oriented, for example, local labor cost, availability of workers and their know-how, and access to roads, airports, and railroads (Abele et al. 2008; Stevenson 2015).

In essence, the main issue for selecting a location is the expected productivity of that location. The main concerns for productivity are

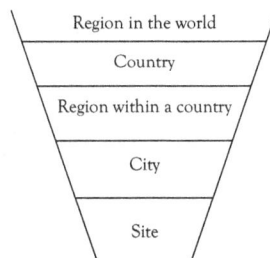

Figure 5.9 Funnel approach toward location decision

different for different types of facilities. For example, for R&D facilities the availability of professional talent is very important whereas for a manufacturing facility the availability of energy plays a more important role. Factors that play a role in this regard are those mentioned in previous chapters, for instance, the overall environment, for example, working conditions (Steenhuis and de Bruijn 2006) and culture (Steenhuis and de Bruijn 2007), and how this environment helps or hinders productivity improvements. The next set of chapters will provide additional insight. Factors that should also be considered are the vulnerability of the location to national disasters. For example, Japan is a very vulnerable location because it is exposed to several different types of risks such as earthquakes and volcanoes because it is located at the crossing point of three tectonic plates (de Blij 2009). The devastating 2011 earthquake and tsunami that hit Tokyo is the latest example of the risk for this location. Companies can also pick locations with improvement potential. For example, Nissan has located a plant in Sunderland, UK (Herron and Hicks 2008), that was an area with high unemployment due to the demise of traditional industries such as shipbuilding and coal mining. Workers might be more motivated under this type of condition. A similar example is Boeing's new plant in South Carolina. The workforce in South Carolina is not unionized and South Carolina is one of the poorest states in the United States.*

Outsourcing

One popular method for companies to have international involvement is to outsource part or all of their production. In particular if the motive of the company is to have access to low cost production factors, it may consider international outsourcing to suppliers in low-cost countries. Often this means developing and low-labor-cost countries.

When companies move production to outside suppliers, they can use different categories to delineate between types of suppliers. This can be related to the quality requirements, that is, the type of certification that a supplier has. This can be ISO but can also be company specific. For example, the Boeing Commercial Airplane Group had its

---

* www.census.gov

own Advanced Quality System (AQS) certification. Aside from quality requirements, another distinction is the type of supplier, that is, what it supplies. For example, Bombardier Aerospace makes, among others, a distinction between machine and specialty shops, major subcontractors, minor subcontractors, distributors, and ground support equipment suppliers. Another distinction is based on the responsibilities. For example, Bombardier Aerospace Class C Major Subcontractors are authorized to procure from their approved supplier base, to substitute material and who are responsible to select and approve their suppliers, whereas its Class G Minor Subcontractors, which fabricate detail components in accordance with Bombardier or customer supplied drawings, are not authorized to procure raw material, substitute material, nor subcontract.

Outsourcing has often been viewed as an excellent method to reduce cost and some studies have shown considerable savings. For example, one study found that 88 percent of the firms that used worldwide sourcing reported a purchase price decline and that the average purchase price declined by 15 percent (Trent and Monczka 2003). Despite this type of evidence, several studies have indicated that there are conflicting findings related to outsourcing benefits (Görg, Hanley, and Strobl 2008; Kitcher et al. 2013; McCann 2011; Meixell, Kenyon, and Westfall 2014). Companies often do not include all relevant costs in their outsourcing decision (Song, Platts, and Bance 2007), but more importantly outsourcing is not just a matter of cost (Dekkers 2011), that is, the results should be viewed more carefully and go beyond the macro analysis level, that is, average low-labor-cost; see also section *Input Conditions* in Chapter 4. For example, Caddick and Dale (1987) found that suppliers in less developed countries quoted prices that were much higher than macrostudies would suggest and that at least part of this differential was due to lower productivity, that is, a firm in a less developed nation employs three to five times as many people to do a job as would be found in a similar firm in a developed country.

One thing to consider, which also applies when setting up plants in low-labor-cost countries, is that it is often not a strategic move, that is, other companies can do the same, and that the savings in labor can end up costing more due to administrative cost, tariffs, larger inventories, and training employees (Markides and Berg 1988). "The mere fact that a lot of companies are doing it [moving manufacturing offshore] doesn't make it smart" (Markides and Berg 1988, 113). Another study reached similar conclusions, that is, other practices related to the enhancement of manufacturing capability (e.g., investments in higher manufacturing capability) have a much stronger ability to predict improvements in operating performance than outsourcing (Dabhilkar and Bengtsson 2008). Another related strategic issue is that outsourcing or moving production to low-labor-cost countries can lead to a loss of manufacturing capabilities, that is, hollowing out, and the decline of the industrial commons; see also section *Challenges* in Chapter 3. The strategic view also relates to whether there is a need to have production and R&D in close proximity. Creating distance between R&D and manufacturing can create barriers of communication (Wlazlak and Johansson 2014) and important feedback loops may be negatively impacted, which limits the potential for innovation and improvement. Furthermore, the supplier or more generally the nation in which it is located may through upgrading eventually become a competitor as, for example, has happened with the electronics industry (Borrus 1997; Lüthje 2004).

Outsourcing can also have a strong negative impact on a firm's labor productivity. This is explained as being due to effects of opportunism, disturbed competence formation, and of limited innovative value creation processes that may overcompensate cost benefits (Broedner, Kinkel, and Lay 2009). Furthermore, depending upon the type of product that it involves, it might be better to outsource to a supplier in an advanced, that is, high-labor-cost, country than in a developing, that is, low-labor-cost, country. For example, a U.S. company that produces car parts found that domestic outsourcing was the best option, even compared to outsourcing to low-cost countries such as Mexico, India, and China. This was due to transportation cost from low-labor-cost countries but also because shipping often requires more protective packaging and often still results in higher scrap rates than when domestic companies are involved. Also, there may be reputational risks as was discussed in section *Internationalization*.

Another issue to pay attention to is how the financial comparisons of make versus buy are calculated. There are two factors that should be considered in this regard. First, there is the matter of the overhead. Many companies are not precise in cost allocation, that is, they distinguish direct costs as well as indirect costs, that is, overhead. For example Meixell, Kenyon, and Westfall (2014) found that outsourcing increases overhead. One thing that matters in this regard is how the overhead is allocated. This may, for example, be based on a percentage of direct labor cost. Comparing the total cost in this manner for the domestic factory versus outsourcing production to a low-labor-cost country may create an unfavorable picture, which is partly due to the importance attached to the labor cost. In this case, it would be prudent to examine more carefully the overhead at the domestic factory and to determine how much of this overhead would be eliminated by outsourcing the product. For example, if a company uses the direct labor cost as a method for allocating overhead and it produced three products—two highly automated with limited labor involved and one highly labor intensive—then outsourcing the labor-intensive production line would not necessarily lead to a proportionate savings on overhead so that the cost of the other two products would increase due to the disproportionate overhead. In addition, there might be administrative (overhead) cost involved when outsourcing such as staff time to communicate with overseas suppliers, paper cost, and communication costs involved in sending faxes, and so forth. Especially in the case of a company from a linear-active culture outsourcing to a multiactive culture, there is a need for increased communication; see Chapter 2. Other studies have also shown that outsourcing shifts some cost to managing the relationship (Boulaksil and Fransoo 2010; Yang, Wacker, and Sheu 2012). The second factor that should be considered is the plant capacity. This is in essence a similar issue. If a plant decides to outsource, it needs to consider the effect that this has on the utilization and efficiency of the rest of the plant. If, on the one hand, the outsourcing creates freeing of capacity that will be used for the production of other items, then the utilization and efficiency are not necessarily impacted. If, on the other hand, the capacity is not used for other products but remains idle, then the fixed costs will have to be spread over fewer products and thus the cost of the products that remained for domestic production will increase.

All in all, outsourcing may be a good option but it is really import-ant to look at all of the costs involved, including overhead, and the impact outsourcing may have on the rest of the factory. Furthermore, outsourcing or moving production to low-labor-cost countries does not appear to be a strategic solution and although it can lead to cost reduc-tions, in many cases it also leads to cost increases. This can explain why reshoring occurs, see Chapter 1, and may even represent a trend (Kinkel 2012).

Internationalization Implications and in Particular for Outsourcing

This chapter has shown that there are many alternatives for how a com-pany decides to go international. The main points to take away is that despite what may appear in the media, most of the FDI and trade still occur between the developed nations. The channel for internationalization has consequences for the degree of control and the cost of control. For the decision-making process of a plant location, managers typically follow a funnel process as illustrated in Figure 5.9. However, the different chapters in this book point to many additional factors that should be analyzed.

This section will focus specifically on the outsourcing of produc-tion processes. This is because outsourcing has often been viewed as an excellent method to reduce cost but several recent scientific studies have questioned this notion and, for example, many U.S. companies are now reshoring their operations back to the United States. To gain insight and sensitivity in the outsourcing decision, a manager can do the following:

- When considering outsourcing, the first question that should be asked is whether this is really a strategic solution or a tacti-cal move that can easily be duplicated by competitors. If it is not a strategic solution, then the manager needs to determine whether other strategic alternatives are available that enhance the competitiveness and are less likely to be duplicated by competitors, for example, fundamental changes in the pro-duction process or method of organizing work. Toyota kept production limited for a long time to Japan but was interna-tionally successful through the implementation of advanced manufacturing systems such as lean that gave it a competitive advantage.

- When looking at anticipated cost advantages, the following should also be estimated to allow for a broader understanding:
  o Length of logistical process and cost involved.
  o Potential need for higher inventory levels and cost involved.
  o Effect on dependability of deliveries, probability increase for missed deliveries, and opportunity cost related to this.
  o Possibility of exchange rate fluctuations and cost involved.
  o Time required for communication and solving problems with the supplier, supplier training, and so forth and cost involved. This also includes how much the supplier needs to be managed, not necessarily due to supplier competence but rather this goes back to the national culture that was discussed in Chapter 2. A company from a linear-active culture might discover that when outsourcing to a supplier in a multiactive culture, it needs to follow a hands-on approach with frequent communication so that deadlines are met. This takes time and costs money.
  o Effect on domestic operations when part of production is outsourced, for instance, lower utilization, spread of fixed cost over fewer units, misuse of direct labor hours to allocate overhead.

Carefully analyzing the pros and cons of internationalization channels and especially the outsourcing decision is very important. The recent reshoring examples demonstrate that outsourcing is often not the ultimate solution to competitiveness. It is especially important to determine a broad range of financial impacts and to critically evaluate the financial assumptions underlying the decision-making models.

Conclusion

While in the previous chapter the potential for international operations was pointed out, in this chapter the discussion focused on how to internationalize. First, an overview was presented on worldwide developments in trade and FDI. For both of these areas, large increases have been shown for the last 20 years. Much of the trade and FDI has been between the United States, Europe, and Japan. In recent years, China has become a much more important player. Companies can engage internationally in several different ways. Each has pros and cons and much of this relates to issues such as control, cost, and risk. The traditional pattern of internationalization seems to have lost merit in the current circumstances with relatively low transportation and communication cost, as well as more sophisticated communication and transportation capabilities. Nowadays companies exist that from inception operate internationally. Research indicates that there is not a single approach when this involves a plant in another country. The decision-making process in general follows a funnel approach but there are many variables that play a role and their importance depends upon the situation, that is, type of company, type of industry, motive for the plant, and so forth. Lastly, one popular form of international operations, that is, outsourcing, was discussed. Although outsourcing is frequently equated with cost savings, scientific studies have pointed out that other strategic approaches might lead to more beneficial results. It was also pointed out that outsourcing goes beyond the labor cost saved. One of the hidden dangers of outsourcing lies in the accounting reasoning behind the decision. The accounting standards should not be taken for granted but rather in-depth analysis is required to make sure that removing parts of production from a plant does not increase the cost, that is, lower the productivity, of the production that is left behind.

CHAPTER 6

International Practices and Operations Networks

In April 2004, I was on a trip to Cancun in Mexico. On my way there, I had a stop-over at the Benito Juárez International Airport in Mexico City. While at the airport waiting for my connecting flight, I made two observations. First, although my connection time was only a couple of hours, there was no information on the screens with regard to my connecting flight. In fact, this made me rather uncomfortable. As a passenger on flights within Europe and the United States, mostly when you arrive at an airport there are large screens with flight information of flights for the entire day, or so it seems. In any event, flights are scheduled well in advance, gates are assigned in advance, and although not all flights are posted on screens this is mostly an issue of not having enough screen space available. Of course, some of the information is subject to change as flights may be delayed, and so forth, so then gates and departure times can change. In Mexico City, there was only information for a few flights and since I had no idea where my next flight was, I also did not know how far I needed to walk to the departure gate. This created quite some uncertainty for me. Similar observations can be made in Brazil, India, and Italy. For example, in Sao Paulo there were screens that had departure information for later flights that only added to the discomfort! While in Mexico, eventually, I decided to find an area where I had easy access to the screens and started to look outside. This is where I made my second observation. I was sitting right above an area where luggage was being compiled outside. Over the next hour or so, I witnessed how luggage was brought to the area, placed in a specific part of the area, and later on removed again. If you are at a U.S. airport, you might witness the same thing. Well, almost. For example, if you are at a gate at the Chicago O'Hara International Airport you might notice a luggage tug vehicle that has several baggage carts. This tug vehicle might arrive well in advance of the aircraft and drop off carts with luggage for the flight. This is possible because passengers have already checked in their luggage and with the systems in place, that is, departure gates are known, luggage can already be dropped off at the right location to be placed on the aircraft once it arrives. If, for some reason, the gate changes, the little tug vehicles simply pick up all the luggage carts and move them to the new location. At the airport in Mexico City, it was not quite that organized. One difference was that the area I was watching was a general collection area for luggage, that is, not for one gate but for multiple gates. For example, I would see a tug vehicle arrive with luggage carts. The driver would get off the vehicle, walk by the different areas where luggage was placed to check for which flight it was, then eventually find the right *spot* to drop off the luggage. At the time it was not left on carts either but suitcases were taken off the carts and placed on the ground. Then, apparently when an aircraft was ready to be loaded, somebody would search the area for the luggage that belonged to that flight. Luggage was then placed on a cart and the tug vehicle would tow it away. All in all, a considerable amount of time was spent on either finding the luggage for a flight by checking the luggage tags that were spread across the area, or by discussing with others where the luggage of certain flights was held.

The point of this example is that the methods of organizing work can be quite different in different locations. These methods affect the overall productivity of the workforce. For example, the system as it was used in Mexico City at that time was clearly less efficient and less organized than what is typical in the United States. In this chapter, I will cover aspects that relate to operating in a different, that is, international, environment.

International Practices

As was discussed previously, in particular in section *Input Conditions* in Chapter4, productivity of a production process in a specific location is influenced by characteristics of that location. In the following, I will describe three types of practices that affect the productivity of operations: inventory control, management and leadership, and scheduling and method of organizing.

A study on management style found that management style is affected by national culture and that management style is related to productivity (Morris and Pavett 1992). The study examined a U.S. parent plant and a Mexican subsidiary plant. It was found that whereas in the United States companies typically use a participatory management style, in Mexico an authoritative style is more common. Based on their culture, Mexican workers expect an authority figure to make decisions and assume responsibility; see also Chapter 2. Where it gets really interesting is that a comparison of productivity showed that the productivity, measured as direct labor hours per unit, of the U.S. plant and the Mexican plant were statistically the same. What this indicates is that there is not a specific management style that leads to the highest labor productivity, but rather that the management style used has to fit with the national culture. In practical terms, this means that, for instance, if a U.S. company sets up a subsidiary in Mexico, then it has to reconsider whether it should use its U.S. management style. Not recognizing the cultural values, and related to this the appropriate management style, can lead to years of delays when implementing operations in another country, as one company found (Acosta et al. 2004). It also means that expatriates need to be selected that can adjust their behavior consistent with the local cultural values (Shin, Morgeson, and Campion 2007).

Several studies have been conducted on the observed differences in operations practices across countries. A compilation of several studies occurs in Whybark and Vastag (1993). This work continues to be updated through the Global Manufacturing Research Group. These studies indicate that companies use different operations practices in different countries. In several of these studies, operations practices were related to forecasting, production planning and scheduling, shopfloor activities, and purchasing and materials management. Some examples of findings were that there were differences between China and South Korea, which are explained by the degree of state planning that was used in China (Rho and Whybark 1993). Another study found that national culture dimensions such as uncertainty avoidance and individuality are significant predictors of supply chain management decisions and practices such as how many suppliers are used, how much to outsource, whether to export, and the planning horizon of forecasts (Pagell, Katz and Sheu 2005).

In Romania, for example, this type of cultural influence on practices can also be observed. In one instance, a Romanian company that was doing subcontracting work was using a centralized planning approach to inventory, that is, ordering exact amounts of material for each product, whereas the Western-party that had outsourced production to the Romanian supplier was using a decentralized approach with fluctuating inventory levels, that is, replenishing when necessary. These differences in systems are particularly relevant when a company engages in production in another country because the country environment may fit better with certain approaches than with other approaches. Thus, if a company engages in a joint venture it may encounter difficulties with applying the practices that it is used to in the domestic situation. It also plays a role when a company outsources to an international company but is still in control of the production, see also Chapter 5, because the practices used at the domestic plant may be difficult to use for the supplier. Another example of how operations practices can be different and difficult to implement relates to human resources and the scheduling of work. Another implication of these practices can be found in India where scheduling work is much harder than in, for example, the United States. This is because the workforce in India is *unstable*, that is, people do not always show up for work. Under those conditions, it is really difficult to develop a production schedule.

The third type of practice that affects the productivity of operations is the way work is organized. An example was already provided in the introduction of this chapter. Organization was considered by the Technology Atlas Group as an important component of a production technology (Technology Atlas Team 1987; Ramanathan 1994) and needless to say, a good organization can be critical for productivity. However, how work is organized in one country is not necessarily how work is organized in another country, nor is it necessarily easy to transfer. A study on Japanese management practices in Chinese subsidiaries found that their application was limited (Taylor 2001). A study on the application of Kaizen in Dutch subsidiaries of Japanese companies had similar results (Yokozawa and Steenhuis 2013). The explanation for this is that the systems originate in a specific context and that people in a different context and in a different culture may not want or be able to adopt the same systems.

In addition to the practices, the overall environment and working conditions (Steenhuis and de Bruijn 2006) also play an important role; see also section *Input Conditions* in Chapter 4. Furthermore, as explained in Chapter 2, when dealing with a different culture, it may mean that more supervision is required. This creates additional management and control-related costs. This also applies to outsourcing; see section *Plant Location* in Chapter 5.

What this means overall is that when setting up operations in another country (whether through wholly or partially owned subsidiaries or through *controlled* outsourcing), it is important to examine the local operations practice, determine whether the domestic practices will be successful in the international location, and if not, what the effect on productivity will be and how this impacts overall cost.

Global Operations Networks

Once a company deals with one or more factories in one or more countries, it can be considered part of an international operations network. In this section, I will use the term international operations network rather than similar type terms such as global commodity chain, global value chain, and global production network because these have a distinct meaning in academic circles; see, for example, Coe, Dicken, and Hess (2008). The term international operations network covers the meaning of what I will discuss in this section, that is, companies that have international operations connected through a network. With one or more plants in different countries, things can get fairly complex and Figure 6.1 illustrates some of the types of connections that may exist in an international operations network. Figure 6.1 does not illustrate all of the potential international linkages and does not explicitly distinguish different country characteristics such as a high-wage versus a low-wage country. However, it shows several possible relationships that can exist in a global production network. It also illustrates the complexity when all relationships are viewed in combination.

The circle in the middle of country B is the headquarters of the global company. Other circles represent subsidiaries of the company whereas squares represent outside suppliers. This leads to the following possible relationships:

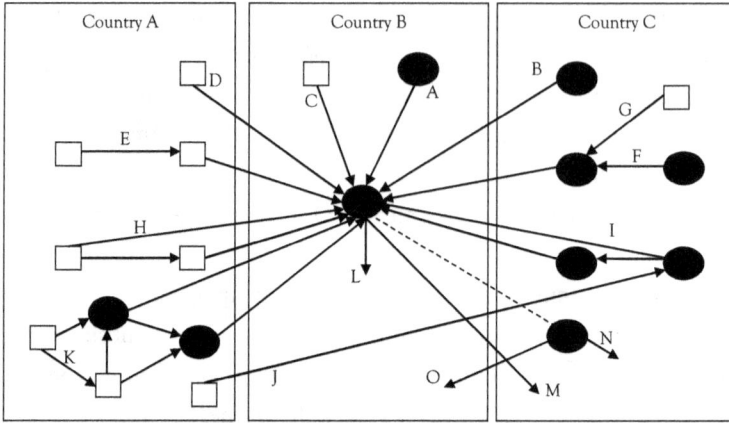

Figure 6.1 International operations network

A, B, C, and D represent the fairly simple relationships between HQ and supplying companies either internal (A and B) or external (C and D) to the company. The suppliers can be in the same country (A and C) or be in other countries (B and D).

Relationships E, F, and G show a little more depth with another tier of suppliers that, again, can be inside or outside the company. In reality, there are typically even more than two tiers of suppliers involved in global production networks. Relationships H and I show a little more complexity where a direct (internal or external) supplier to headquarters can also have an indirect relationship through supplying another supplier that supplies the HQ. Relationship J shows how a similar situation as relationship G but now an outside supplier is located in a different country. Finally relationship K shows a combination of several different types of relationships.

From a slightly different perspective, shown by arrows that do not lead to circles or boxes, are relationships L through O, which show where sales occur. Sales can be domestic by the HQ, as shown by L, or international by the HQ, as shown by M. It is also possible that a more or less independent subsidiary sells to a local market, as shown by N, or even to the domestic market, shown by O.

International operations networks can offer several advantages compared to stand-alone factories, because they have the potential of shifting operations around the network to achieve optimal operations. A key question for international operations networks is: How should they be configured? That means, what kind of factories should there be in the network and where should they be located?

There is no consensus theory on this available but there are some valuable insights with regard to this configuration issue. One insight is related to the overall structure of the international network. Four different types of companies have been distinguished in academic circles (Bartlett and Ghoshal 2002) although in practice the terms are often used interchangeably. Global companies are companies that take advantage of economies of scale. That is, they have centralized operations (R&D and production in one or a limited number of locations) and sell the same products internationally. Japanese companies such as Toyota traditionally followed this approach and had very limited production outside of Japan. Multinational companies are companies that are primarily aimed at local responsiveness. That is, they have decentralized operations where different products are produced locally for local markets. European companies such as Unilever have traditionally followed this approach. International companies are companies that have capitalized on knowledge transfer. That is, to some degree they are decentralized similar to multinational companies to allow for local adaptation but the headquarters has a more involved role in particular in R&D and knowledge is shared across the network. Many U.S. companies have followed this model. Transnational companies are the most complex and are aimed simultaneously at lowest cost and highest responsiveness for local differences by spreading production across countries, that is, wherever it makes the most economical sense. In addition to these more western-oriented ways of organizing and thinking about organizing, there are also some other forms. For example, there are types of organizations, which often function internationally, such as the Chaebol, a form of conglomerate from South Korea, and the Keiretsu, a system of groups of companies where companies have small ownership in the other companies from Japan.

Another insight into the overall network perspective relates to the combination of how geographically dispersed the manufacturing operations are and how coordination takes place between international manufacturing operations (Shi and Gregory 1998). This led to seven different types of international manufacturing network configurations. Three of these are multidomestic manufacturing configurations with an increasing degree of plant dispersion. These configurations are tailored to the local market and have autonomy. The remaining four are global manufacturing configurations with increasing degree of plant dispersion. These are globally oriented featured with integration and coordination across the networks. This can be a global company, international company, or transnational company in terms of the preceding discussion.

These two insights are valuable as they provide us with a tool to categorize an international operations network. However, they are limited in terms of providing guidelines with regard to how to set up the networks in the most productive manner. In this regard, research by Ferdows (1997b) provides meaningful insight. Ferdows (1997b) looked at the reason for the plant's existence and the competency level at the plant. Ferdows (1997b) found, and later Vereecke and van Dierdonck (2002) confirmed, that companies generally have three primary motives for setting up foreign subsidiaries. The three primary motives are: proximity to markets, proximity to skills and knowledge, and access to low-cost production factors such as low labor cost or raw materials; see also Chapter 4. Based on the primary motive and the site competence, Ferdows (1997b) distinguishes six roles of foreign factories based on the primary motive for the plant and the competence level of the plant; see Figure 6.2.

The contributor and server plants are primarily established to be close to the market. The difference is that the contributor plant has more technical expertise. The source and offshore plants are primarily

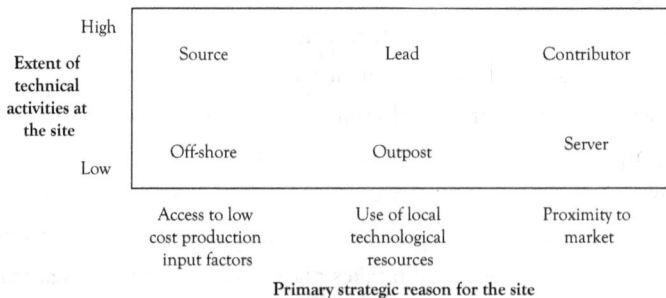

High	Source	Lead	Contributor
	Off-shore	Outpost	Server
Low			

Extent of technical activities at the site

Access to low cost production input factors	Use of local technological resources	Proximity to market

Primary strategic reason for the site

Figure 6.2 Roles of factories

Source: Adapted from Ferdows (1989).

established for access to lower production costs and the source plant has more technical expertise. Lastly, the lead and outpost plants are primarily established to have access to knowledge and skills where the lead plant has the more technical expertise. Note that companies do not always have only one motive to set up a plant. An example is the Electrolux plant in Jászberény, Hungary. Electrolux invested in this plant in 1991 and among other things this plant produced vacuum cleaners, refrigerators, and freezers. Hungary not only offered a low-cost production site to Electrolux, but it also provided proximity to the Eastern European market.

When looking at the long-term stability of the factories, in line with the notion that average wages in countries tend to develop over time (see section *Economic Strategies*), the factories that are established for cost reasons are the least stable in the long term. Over a 10-year period from 1995 to 2005, a study found that only 33 percent of the factories established for cost reasons survived whereas almost 80 percent of the factories established to serve the local market and over 85 percent of factories established to get access to skills or knowledge survived (Vereecke, De Meyer, and van Dierdonck 2008).

A slightly different, complementary, view on plant roles was developed based on how much interaction takes place between a plant and other plants in the network in terms of the frequency of communication of the plant with other plants, the innovation flows to and from the plant, and the flow of visitors to and from the plant (Vereecke, van Dierdonck and De Meyer 2006). This led to four types of plants. Two types of plants are not very active in the network. The *isolated plant* is relatively young, market focused, has little inflow and outflow of components and semifinished goods, a relatively low level of strategic autonomy in plant design, and a relatively high level of managerial investment. The *receiver plant* is also relatively young, has relatively little outflow of components and semifinished goods, has a relatively low level of managerial investment, and a relatively low level of capabilities. The two other types of plants are network players. The *hosting network player* is relatively old, serves a broad market, has a high inflow of components and semifinished goods, and a relatively low level of managerial investment. Lastly, the *active network player* has a high inflow and outflow of components and semi-finished goods, a relatively high level of strategic autonomy in plant design, and a relatively high level of process investment.

In light of the preceding discussion, it is useful to distinguish different types of production activities that can be moved within the international operations network. It makes sense to distinguish simple production activities, more complex production activities, and assembly line activities. Logically, within the international operations network, simple production activities can be moved relatively easily to other, cheaper, locations whereas more complex production activities might require an environment that has higher skill levels and assembly activities might be placed closer to the market. For example, take the textile industry. Compared to developing nations, German firms have greater complexity in technical design, use higher quality of fabrics, and trim and cater mostly to the upper middle market with an emphasis on quality, fit, and often brand (Lane and Probert 2006).

Whether this is, strictly, how production is moved around in an international operations network depends upon two opposing influences. It depends on whether there is a need or push for concentrating production in one or limited locations and whether there is a need or push for dispersing production in multiple locations. Abele et al. (2008) examined this and identified two dimensions. One dimension relates to the production cost and examines whether there are economies of scale and scope that push for the concentration of production. The other dimension relates to the market and the need to be in close proximity due to the need for local adaptation. In addition, the element of transaction cost plays a role. This includes, for example, logistics costs. What matters in this regard is the relative cost of transportation compared to the overall product cost. A high relative cost of transportation and a need for local adaptation push for a dispersion of activities. An indicator that provides insight into the relative cost of transportation is the value density, that is, the value per unit of weight. If the value density is high then the transportation cost is a comparatively low percentage whereas if the value density is low, then the transportation cost is a comparatively high percentage of overall cost.

Based on these two dimensions, Abele et al. (2008) identified five different types of production networks, that is, world factory, local for local, sequential or convergent, hub and spoke, and web structure.

This insight of different operations networks allows integration with some of the previously discussed concepts. The five operations network types are shown in Figure 6.3. There is a distinction between on the one hand the world factory and the local for local operations networks and on the other hand the sequential or convergent, hub and spoke, and web structure operations networks. For the latter three types, there is more separation of parts of the production process. This is why the terms multidomestic and global are placed in Figure 6.3, because two of the types fit with the description of these types of companies as described earlier. The terms transnational and international are not used in Figure 6.3 because they are based on different perspectives and do not align well. The transnational company can apply to all three of the remaining operations network types. The international company does not fit specifically with these identified types of international operations networks because it relates more to knowledge flows, which is not an explicit dimension in Figure 6.3. Figure 6.3 also shows some of the plant types because of some of the overlap.

The traditional model of the global company is similar to the notion of a world factory and also fits with the description of a lead factory. This is a relatively simple network structure in terms of plants and their roles. In this case, there is only one, lead, factory that supplies the entire world market. There is therefore only a flow of products from the factory to the customers. Products that can be produced this way have high economies of scale, a low need for local adaptation, and normally have a high value density. An example is aircraft production. For aircraft, it

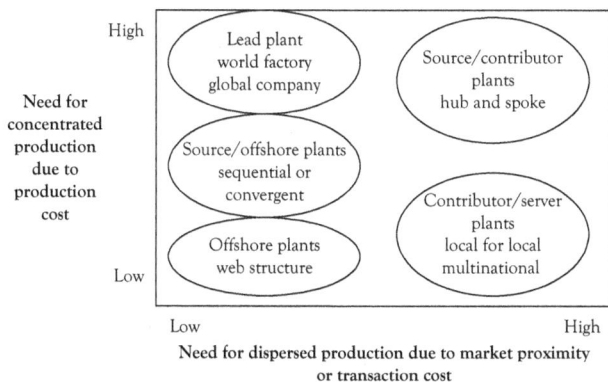

Figure 6.3 Integration of several international operations network related concepts

is not very typical to have multiple plants producing the same product although in recent years a few duplicate production lines have actually been set up. Some of this has to do with gaining access to a local market. For example, as a joint venture between Airbus and a Chinese consortium of Tianjin Free Trade Zone (TJFTZ) and China Aviation Industry Corporation (AVIC), a second A320 final assembly line in Tianjin, China, began operations in September 2008. The other A320 assembly line is in Toulouse, France. Another reason that has been identified as influencing a company's decision to move manufacturing is the influence of labor and unions; see, for example, Ietto-Gillies (1992). This seems to have been largely the motivation for Boeing to set up a nonunionized Boeing 787 plant in North Charleston, South Carolina, in October 2009 after experiencing a 58-day strike in 2008, which is estimated as having cost Boeing $1.8 billion in losses.

The other traditional model is the local for local system. In this case there are smaller economies of scale and a high need for local adaptation. This is similar in concept to the multinational company, in which factories exist that supply regions. This is also a relatively straightforward model in terms of plant roles. In this case, the plant roles are linked to proximity to market. Thus, most of the plants in this type of network are contributor or server plants. Unilever was mentioned earlier as an example of this type of multinational company. It is now relatively easy to see why Unilever would follow this particular network approach. For example, for its shampoo products there are some economies of scale and scope but considering the overall market size, that is, volume of production, these economies can be achieved within several factories, that is, there is no need to have only one world factory. Also, there is some need for local adaption, for example, because of different types of packaging (different languages on the labels, different sizes of the shampoo product as discussed in Chapter 2). Furthermore, the value density of shampoo is relatively low and thus the cost for transporting shampoo is relatively high compared to the value of the product, and hence a local for local approach makes more sense. Similar network structures apply to other types of products such as beverages.

The sequential or convergent network structure is mostly based on achieving economies of scale and scope, and there is less need for local adaptation for the products involved in this production network. This means that it is mainly oriented on the cost of production. For this reason, the source and offshore factories are placed in this network in Figure 6.3 although other types of plants are also part of this network. In the sequential or convergent network, manufacturing of different parts and components is concentrated in a different location. Thus, for example, the production of simple parts can take place in a low-labor-cost country, and the production of more complex parts can take place in a higher-labor-cost country where the skills and expertise are available for this task. This network type involves a high amount of transportation and therefore is only practical for high value density products. An example of this is a smartphone.

Hub and spoke system is similar to the sequential or convergent network structure but the difference is that it is organized in such a manner that it can achieve both economies of scale and scope (by concentrating manufacturing in specific locations) as well as achieving the possibility of local adaptation (by having sites that are close to the market). This is accomplished by having the production of parts and components in appropriate locations while assembly is taking place close to the market. In Figure 6.3, this is shown by the placement of the source plant, for low cost, and contributor plant, for proximity to market, in this network type. In this instance, there is a high amount of transportation of parts and complex components, which tend to have a higher value density and often face lower customs duties. For example Volvo trucks has used this type of structure where parts have been produced in a number of countries such as Peru, Australia, Iran, and Malaysia, engine production has been concentrated in Belgium, Brazil, and Sweden, and major assembly of trucks occurred in the United States, Belgium, and Sweden, while the R&D was mainly conducted in Sweden. Another example of this is the Mercedes Benz plant located in Pune, India, that was mentioned in Chapter 2. In this instance assembly took place in Pune, India, whereas parts were imported from other regions.

The last model, the web structure, is the most complex in terms of coordination, and in this regard I have equated it with the transnational company. The web structure is the most flexible of all the network types. All products can be produced in all factories and allocation of production takes place based upon available capacity, and so forth. It is possible in this network that a plant in the United States supplies customers in Europe while a plant in Europe supplies customers in the United States; this depends on, for example, the timing of the orders. Due to the large amount of transportation, this network type is only appropriate for products that have at least a moderate to high value density. This type of system allows for much transfer of learning to other factories within the network. Another potential advantage of this network type is that it can create internal competition for orders. Internal competition can motivate companies to be innovative, that is, improve products or production processes, which leads to overall productivity improvements.

Estimating the Impact of International Networks on the Productivity

Whereas in Chapter 4 the impact of the general environment was addressed, in this chapter more operations-specific aspects were addressed. The main point to take away is that companies need to realize how the practices that are commonly used in their domestic plant may not be the most appropriate in other countries. It is also important to consider which type of international operations network is the most appropriate and the role of each plant in that network. To gain insight and sensitivity into the influence of the country environment (including the national culture) on the operations practices, a manager can do the following:

- First, the manager needs to determine the operations practices at the domestic location. Operations should be viewed broadly and include topics such as inventory control (for parts, components, and final products), scheduling practices, forecasting methods, and management and leadership approaches. This provides insight into how the company operates in its domestic location. Many of these practices will be common across companies in the same domestic country and will, for example, be taught in domestic business schools.
- Next, the manager needs to determine the operations practices of companies at the international location. This means

assessing how the same practices are typically done and, for example, what practices are taught at business schools.

- Once the practices in the domestic location as well as in the international location are understood, an assessment needs to be made of the impact of differences between the domestic operations practices and the international operations practices. This assessment needs to cover at least two different perspectives. One perspective is where the company adjusts its domestic operations practices and changes them in the international location to what is already familiar in that location. The other perspective is where the company maintains its domestic operations practices and thus people at the international location have to change the operations practices and what they are familiar with. For example, if at the domestic home location a typical inventory approach is to use a decentralized inventory approach with fluctuating inventory levels but a common practice in the international location is to use a centralized approach and exact amounts of material are used, then an assessment needs to be made about how each of these approaches influences the cost and timeliness of operations.

- Finally, a plan should be developed to deal with the differences and the cost and timing of this plan needs to be assessed. For example, a new inventory approach might have to be introduced in the international location. This can involve training of employees as well as changing administrative systems, channels of communication, and so forth.

It is extremely important to assess the difference in operations practices and to estimate their impact. This is often overlooked and underestimated precisely because these practices are so common in the domestic location and often there is limited awareness of why the practices should be conducted differently because they are widely established and considered the best and proven in the domestic location. This is also very much connected to the national culture that was discussed in Chapter 2.

Another aspect that was discussed in this chapter was the configuration of international operations networks. The main point to take away is that there are many different configuration options and when dealing with global networks there are many complexities. To gain insight and sensitivity into how to design an international operations network, a manager can do the following:

- First, the need for multiple plants due to market proximity and transaction cost needs to be assessed. The market proximity aspect is related to the demand in the international location and the need to be in close proximity and adapt the product to local conditions. This relates to conditions such as the national culture and other environment conditions as discussed in Chapters 2 and 4. Transaction costs are influenced by, for example, the cost of transportation and thus the value density of the products needs to be assessed. A low value density is an indication that multiple plants might be a desirable configuration.
- Second, the need for multiple plants due to the production cost and, for example, economies of scale needs to be assessed. For instance, it is necessary to have very large plants or is a combination of smaller plants a feasible alternative?
- Based on both preceding aspects, the ideal network configuration needs to be established. Depending upon this ideal network configuration and complexity, the cost and efforts of coordinating the network should also be assessed because although these costs are not attributable to any single factory, they influence overall operations.
- Next, the specific role of the international factory within the network needs to be determined. This is connected with the primary strategic reason for the plant (also discussed in Chapter 5) and with the assessment of the type of economy and environment as discussed in Chapters 3 and 4. For instance, in the case of factor-driven economies the offshore plant (low-cost production) or the server plant (proximity to market) are the most feasible types of plants.

It is important for an operations manager to determine the ideal network configuration as well as the role of the plant within that network. This is because the network configuration not only has an impact on the overall cost and productivity of operations but more importantly it connects with other aspects such as flexibility, dependability, and speed of operations. For improvement of the network overall, an assessment can be made about how the plants in the network might change roles based upon upgrading of plants. Furthermore, the network might be expanded, for example, as new markets open up, it might be changed as low-cost production locations change or exchange rates change, and so forth. In other words, the operations manager needs to be continuously aware of the changing international (economic) environment.

Conclusion

In this chapter the focus shifted to international operations networks. There are two primary concerns when a company establishes operations facilities in different countries. The first concern is the productivity of an individual plant. This plays a role when a wholly or partially owned foreign subsidiary is created but also in instances of outsourcing where the company maintains a large degree of control. The issue is that productivity of the plant is related to its overall cost structure. The cost of production at an individual plant is partially influenced by the labor cost. This is typically viewed in terms of wages per hour hence terms such as low-labor cost country. Another big part of the overall cost relates to how productive the plant is which goes back to the discussion in previous chapters. This relates to issues of operations practices, leadership, and how work is organized. These aspects, as it turns out, are influenced by local circumstances such as the prevailing national culture. Leadership practices differ across the world and a practice that leads to the most productive results in one country may not be the best approach in another country. One of the challenges faced by companies is to determine what is appropriate for a particular location, what the effect of it will be on overall levels of productivity, and whether it can adapt different approaches in different locations within its overall operations network.

The second concern is the productivity of the overall operations network. Operations networks consist of a range of plants that serve different purposes. The issue here is that productivity of the overall operations network can be enhanced by having plants with appropriate roles and an overall network structure that is appropriate considering the circumstances. Important circumstances to consider in this regard are the necessity to achieve economies of scale and scope for production. In this regard, production needs to be analyzed across the entire chain, that is, it is possible that some parts have economies of scale while other components may not have economies of scale. This determines the need for concentrated production. Another set of important circumstances relate to the need to adapt to the local market and the transaction cost involved in this. For example, a high need for local adaptations pushes the system toward dispersion of activities. The value density of products play an important role in determining the most optimal and productive network structure as this influences the relative transportation costs. Another important factor is the cost in coordinating the network. This is covered in Chapter 7.

CHAPTER 7

Transferring Operations

The need and complexities of transferring operations across several different plants became very clear to me in 1998 while I was working at an aircraft production plant in Romania. A Canadian manufacturer of aircraft had outsourced some of its production to a Romanian company. This was mostly for cost reasons. The part that was produced in Romania was a cockpit. The international operations network at that time could be considered a sequential or convergent network while the Romanian plant could be considered an offshore plant because it had limited responsibilities. At that time, the Romanian company was not allowed to further subcontract any work and it had to follow the Canadian production methods. The Canadian company supplied the Romanian company with the drawings for the cockpit, with process planning sheets that detailed how the cockpit was supposed to be produced and with process specifications, that is, specifications that spell out exactly how a certain type of activity is to be performed. For example, this contained specific instructions on how to do riveting, what kind of rivets to use, and so forth. Different companies can have different procedures so when work is outsourced in this industry, and if the supplier does not have much freedom to follow their own processes, then it is necessary that the supplier familiarizes themselves with the processes of the customer. While manufacturing the cockpit, a problem occurred. The process specifications called for a tube that had to be pushed through a hole in the cockpit wall. Only, there was no hole in the cockpit wall. Subsequent analysis showed that in process planning sheets there were no instructions for drilling a hole in the cockpit wall. Without a hole in the cockpit wall, it is impossible to push a tube through it. Now, you may think that this is not such a big deal, that is, just get a drill and drill a hole.

However, that is not how things work, and certainly not in aviation. If a supplier has to produce an item according to specifications, then it has to be done that way. If the supplier deviates, there are issues of liability. If the process specifications are not up-to-date, then this means that they have to be changed. In this case it meant that contact needed to be made with the customer, that is, the company in Canada. The first issue in this regard was that the company was 7 hours behind, so communication from Romania had to wait until they started working in Canada. This left only a few more hours of the workday in Romania and without a quick response from Canada it took at least another day before a solution was found. Furthermore, it required additional work in Canada to update the process planning sheets. Since this was not a new aircraft, you may wonder how this mistake had gone undetected so far. The reason for this is that initially the cockpit was produced in Canada. At the Canadian plant with this type of problem, it is relatively easy for operations or a shopfloor manager to contact the design department and ask what to do. Since updating process planning sheets is a time-consuming process, other work is sometimes more important, and the solution might be relatively simple, the result may be an oral agreement without a written change so that the manufacturing processes at the plant do not strictly conform to written specifications anymore.

Companies often are not even aware of this until they outsource the job to a supplier that has to conform to specifications. At that point the design (drawings, process planning sheets, and so forth) needs to be updated and increased communication and coordination is required to solve the surprise problem. These are unanticipated costs that are part of the transfer of operations.

Once a company has plants in several different countries (including subcontractors depending upon how much control they have) one of the difficulties is how to coordinate among all of these plants. Two of the international operations networks that were introduced in Chapter 6 are relatively simple: the world factory network and the local for local network. This is because in these instances they operate more as autonomous units although knowledge transfer may still take place between these plants. The other three forms of international operations networks are more complicated because they deal with portions of production processes that take place in different countries. In addition, for the web structure, production is shifted among the different plants according to available capacity, and so forth, which requires even more coordination. This points toward the need to shift production among plants in the international operations network. In this regard, manufacturing mobility, that is, the ability to swiftly transfer production to other plants in the network, has been identified as a key capability for international operations networks (Shi and Gregory 1998).

Time Zone Differences

A first issue to consider, which is mostly absent from scientific studies, is the impact of time zone differences on the coordination across plants in an international operations network.

Figure 7.1 illustrates that if a Seattle-based company has plants in Paris as well as in Shanghai, then there are some challenges with the time available for coordination. Assuming a working day between 8 a.m. and 6 p.m., there will only be 1 hour of overlap between the Seattle company and the Paris plant at the beginning of the day in Seattle (8 to 9 a.m., which is 5 to 6 p.m. in Paris) and 1 hour of overlap between the Seattle company and the Shanghai plant at the end of the day (5 to 6 p.m., which is 8 to 9 a.m. the next day in Shanghai). This is a very limited time and often people may have to work at odd hours to manage problems across the network. The ability to communicate with plants in other geographic areas is also affected by the available communication infrastructure, that is, availability of internet, phone, or fax. Many locations in the world, especially developing nations, have limited availability of these means of communication and even if they exist, they might not be reliable. In addition to communication across plants, a major issue is transferring operations to other plants. This is the main topic for this chapter.

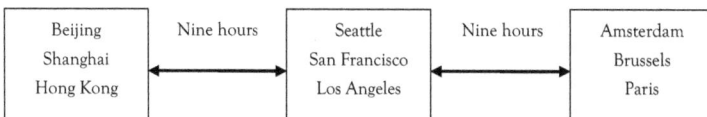

Beijing Shanghai Hong Kong	Nine hours	Seattle San Francisco Los Angeles	Nine hours	Amsterdam Brussels Paris

Figure 7.1 Illustration of time-zone differences

Transferring Technology between Plants

The understanding of how production technology transfer takes place has evolved in the last couple of decades. Initially, the idea was that a technology could be seen as a package. Technology transfer was viewed as picking up the technology and moving it somewhere else as is illustrated in Figure 7.2.

This view of technology transfer did not work well and, for example, did not explain many of the difficulties that were encountered. A more sophisticated view was then developed. In this view, there were some host dependencies. The analogy was that of a person throwing a ball to another person (Grant 1999) as is illustrated in Figure 7.3. In this situation, you have to consider whether the catcher is ready to receive the ball. This, for example, relates to the absorptive capacity of the receiver as well as to the selection of appropriate technologies to transfer.

Even with this viewpoint, there still were problems and some difficulties with technology transfer that could not be explained. This led to another view of technology transfer, that is, the analogy with an organ transplant, see Figure 7.4. In this viewpoint, there are not only host dependencies but also an explicit recognition of home dependencies. That

Figure 7.2 *Traditional view of technology transfer: pick up and place elsewhere*

Figure 7.3 *Adjusted view of technology transfer: able and ready to receive*

means, when a technology is transferred you have to carefully examine where the technology originated because its functioning, that is, productivity, is based on that environment and bringing that technology into a different environment did not guarantee the same level of functioning. In fact, it does not function at all if the two environments are too different.

In more detail, this view is shown in Figure 7.5, the technology transfer balance, indicating that there needs to be some balance, that is, similarity, between the source and destination locations. At the core of Figure 7.5 is the production technology (P). Since the production or manufacturing technology is at the core of Figure 7.5, it is important to explain a little more what a manufacturing technology is. This is especially important when the technology is considered for transfer within an international operations network (see Chapter 6), because in that situation it is important to understand how to transfer the technology and this requires understanding the technology itself. A detailed representation of

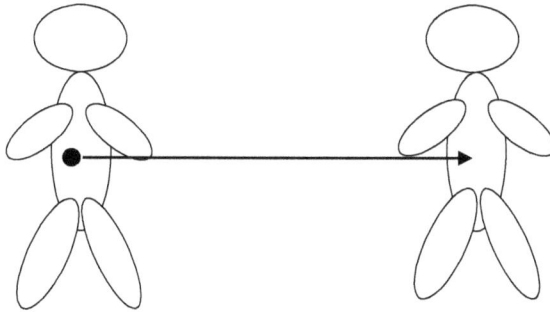

Figure 7.4 More realistic view of technology transfer: transplanting an organ

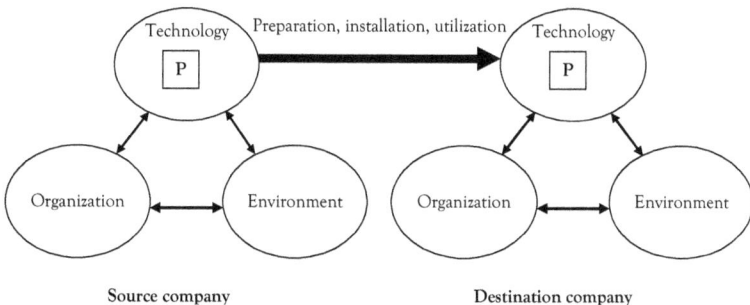

Figure 7.5 Technology transfer balance

Source: Adapted from Steenhuis and de Bruijn (2001).

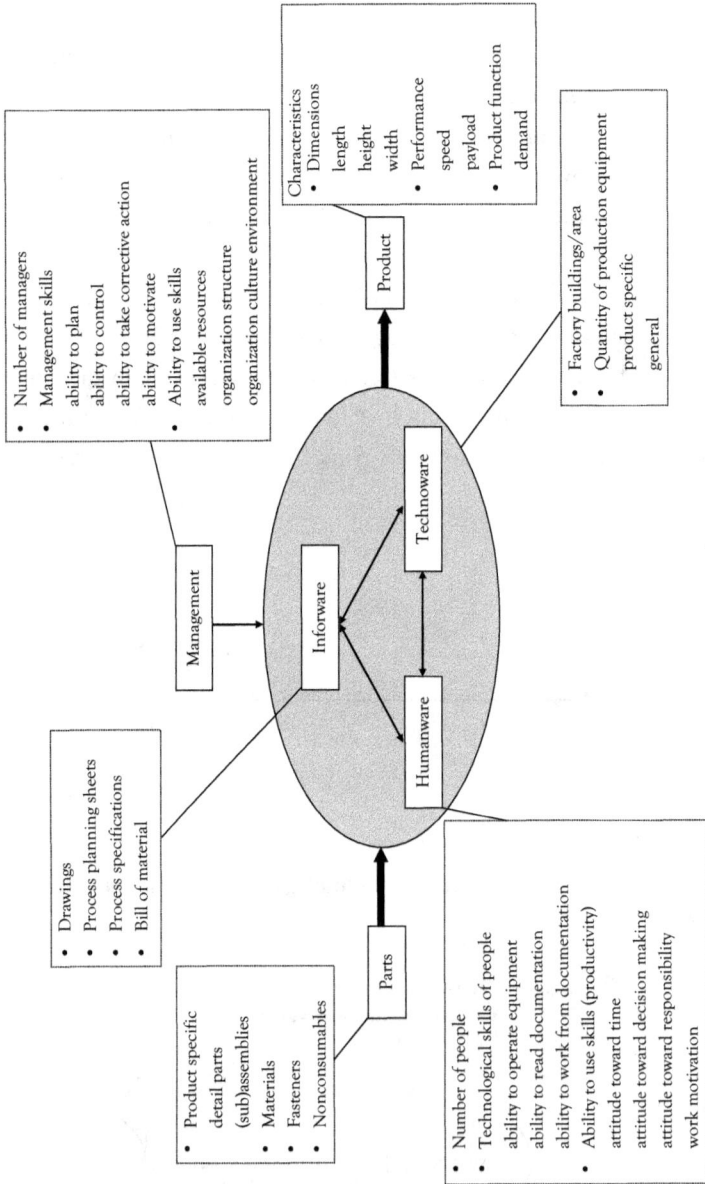

Figure 7.6 Aircraft production technology

a manufacturing technology is shown in Figure 7.6. Figure 7.6 represents aircraft manufacturing technology that relates in particular to the product characteristics but otherwise is a general model.

The (aircraft) production technology consists of know-how (inforware) and means (humanware and technoware) for producing aircraft. Technoware contains the *hardware* for producing the product and humanware the *software* for producing the product. Inforware contains the documentation that is needed for production. The combination of these technology components has to be approved in the aviation industry. Management is required in order to achieve that the technology is utilized productively.

As illustrated by Figure 7.5, the definition of (aircraft) production technology cannot be viewed as an isolated matter. There are three groups of factors that influenced the technology as it exists at the source company: technological factors, organizational factors, and environmental factors. In the section *The Learning Curve*, a particular aspect of an organization will be discussed.

Technological Factors

The technological factors are the size of the technology and its age. The size of a technology is determined by the different technological components as defined in the aircraft production technology definition (Figure 7.6). A large technology such as an assembly line for a car is more difficult and time consuming to transfer than a small technology such as the production of a car door. For example, transferring the production line of a 100-seat aircraft can easily take a decade. In case a technology is very large, it is an option to transfer it in parts. The transfer of detail parts production is technologically more difficult than the transfer of assembly work. The transfer of assembly work is in general logistically more difficult (it is more difficult to keep track of all the detail parts) than the transfer of detail parts production.

The age of a production technology is the elapsed time since the first product was produced. If a technology is derived from an earlier type then it is older, because it relates back to the original technology. The age of a technology has several implications. First, the age of a technology is linked to the demand for the product. The aging of a technology can be a driving factor for a company to sell it, for instance through a license. Second, the age of a technology is related to its condition. Over time, a technology deteriorates. In particular, the condition of the technoware and inforware is important. An old technology will have older, worn out technoware that requires replacement.

In terms of inforware, a new technology will be unstable. This means that the design has not stabilized yet but changes as a result of market feedback, and therefore the inforware is subject to change. An old technology has a more stable inforware component, but at the same time, the older a technology the more shopfloor practice it has—that is production takes place not in compliance with the design. This occurs because operators at the shopfloor come up with improvements, and so forth, but these are not necessarily incorporated into *official* design changes because this is expensive and the operator may not communicate with engineers about this due to organizational barriers. As a consequence, the inforware is not *up-to-date*. This was described in the opening example of this chapter. The implication is that no matter the age of a technology, the inforware will never be completely reliable.

Organizational Factors

The organizational factors are the capacity of an organization, the capability of an organization, and the efficiency of an organization. The capacity of an organization relates to the size, that is, the number of machines and the capacity of each machine, and the number of employees and the capacity of each individual. The maximum capacity of an organization is not the same as the *normal* capacity. For example, under pressure, an organization can require people to work overtime.

The capability of an organization relates to the level of sophistication of products it can deliver. This is determined by the sophistication of the equipment and the skill level of the employees. The latter is related to their knowledge level. The knowledge level relates to an *absolute* knowledge level and a *relative* knowledge level. The *absolute* knowledge level is the knowledge about manufacturing processes and procedures. The *relative* knowledge level is the knowledge about the processes and procedures of other companies. This is important since it provides an indication of the likelihood of misinterpretations. The combination of the capacity and the capability of an organization determine what can be produced and when. If a technology is transferred from one organization to another, the destination company needs to have sufficient capacity and capability to be able to fabricate the product. If not, investments are needed to upgrade the existing capacity and capability. This connects with the concept of absorptive capacity that was previously discussed (see also Jabar, Soosay, and Santa 2011; Whangthomkum, Igel, and Speece 2006).

The efficiency of an organization determines the amount of input an organization requires in order to achieve a certain output. The efficiency of an organization is determined by several factors—first, the organizational structure. This is the manner in which tasks are subdivided and the determination of the power to take decisions. The organizational structure is important because it shows the division of work and the method of decision making. A different organizational structure leads to a different efficiency of an organization. Consequently, transferring a production technology to an organization with a different organizational structure will lead to a different efficiency. Second is the management caliber. This is the extent of the knowledge and skills of the management. It is important because it indicates how well the organization is managed. If the management caliber is low, the efficiency of the organization is likely to be negatively influenced. Third is the organizational culture. This relates to items such as acceptance of responsibility, motivation of the workforce, and attitude toward risk. If employees are not willing to accept responsibility, the efficiency tends to be low. Much time is wasted on formal decision making and allocating responsibilities. If employees are not motivated, their attitude toward their work becomes lax, which can lead to mistakes. The factor attitude toward risk is one that is related to individuals in the organization (acceptance of responsibility) and to the overall organization. To limit the risk in technology transfer, some companies initially use a dual source strategy, that is, they have two suppliers for the same part. Fourth, we have the production methods. This relates to the production philosophy, the difference in production lead time and the delivery interval, and the position on the learning curve. All of these affect the efficiency of an organization. Differences in production philosophy lead to different input requirements and consequently different efficiencies.

The optimum use of resources for production is shown by an alignment of production (workstation) lead times and the delivery interval. When technology is transferred, a loss of efficiency is likely to occur due to the learning curve effects (Steenhuis and de Bruijn 2002), see section *The Learning Curve*. The availability of finances (liquidity) also influences the efficiency of an organization. If liquid assets are not available then the progress can be severely limited. For example, a lack of finances can bring production to a complete stop because it might prohibit the purchase of required production inputs. Fifth, the priority of the technology transfer to an organization is another important influencing factor on the efficiency of an organization. The importance of the program to the source company is of particular importance for the efficiency of the destination company. This is because in many cases there are technical issues that need to be resolved and that require cooperation from the source company. If the source company places a low emphasis on the project and, as a consequence, is negligent in solving technical problems, then the production at the destination company is affected. Sixth, the location of an organization links the organization to its environment. It usually determines the language used (there might be a language barrier between a source company and a destination company) and, as was already pointed out earlier, there might be time zone differences that affect the ease of communication between the two organizations.

Learning Curve

The learning curve principle is an important tool for negotiation with suppliers and for scheduling purposes. It is, for example, widely used in the aircraft industry and applies to other industries as well. It goes beyond the scope of this book to provide a technical explanation of the learning curve or, a related concept, the experience curve, but what will be discussed are its implications. The key idea behind the learning curve is that with human involvement, repetition of tasks leads to productivity improvements. Based on studies in many industries it has been established that for every doubling of production, a constant percentage reduction in time has been observed, and this is termed the learning curve. For example, if the first unit of a production line takes 100 hours to complete, then with an 80 percent curve, the second unit (doubling of production) takes only 80 percent of the first unit, that is, 80 hours. The next doubling of production, that is, the fourth unit, takes only 80 percent of the 80 hours, that is, 64 hours. Doubling again leads to 80 percent of 64 hours, which is 51.2 hours for the eighth unit. In other words, the further one is on the learning curve, the better the efficiency of the organization (people will work faster and need less time to look up what to do). A fully automated line does not experience any type of learning and thus has a 100 percent learning curve, that is, every doubling of production leads to the same time requirement. Depending on the type of product that is produced, a production line stabilizes so that after a certain point no more learning benefits are achieved. An 85 percent learning curve is illustrated in Figure 7.7.

When a technology is transferred from an organization that has already been producing the product to another organization, either to another internal plant or by means of outsourcing, a loss of efficiency will occur due to the learning curve effect. In other words, the destination company will be less efficient than the source company. Figure 7.8 provides a schematic illustration.

The top half of Figure 7.8 relates to the source company and it shows the learning curve that the source company is experiencing. The bottom

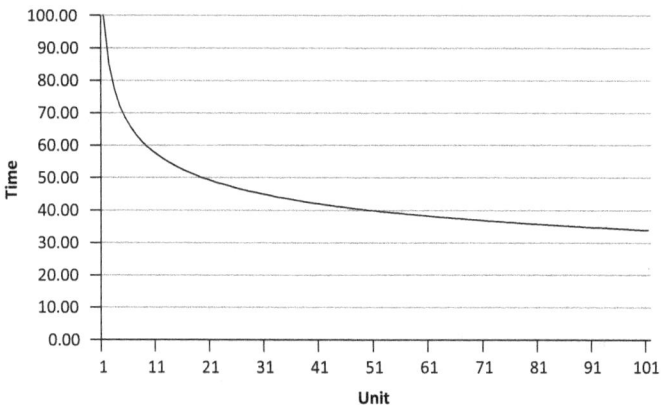

Figure 7.7 An 85% learning curve

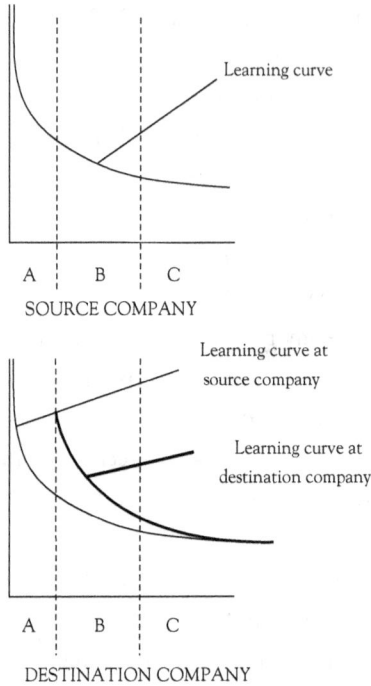

Figure 7.8 Loss of learning when transferring

half of Figure 7.8 relates to the destination company. Three stages are identified in the transfer of production. In the first stage, stage A, the source
company is producing the product. In the second stage, stage B, transfer
takes place, and while the source company is still producing (this facilitates
training opportunities and building a buffer inventory) the destination
company is learning how to produce. In the third stage, stage C, only the
destination company is producing. To enhance the discussion, the source
company's learning curve is copied in the bottom half of the figure. This
source company's curve is shown as continuing in stage C to illustrate that
it would have had additional learning had it continued to produce.

At the start of stage B, the destination company will be less efficient
than the source company. This is because the operations will be unfamil-
iar with the technology and will therefore need to look up information,
and so forth, that operators at the source company do not need to look
up anymore. However, the destination company will not start all the way

at the top of the curve again because some of the learning that occurred at the source company can be transferred to the destination company through, for example, improved process design. If the destination company has a similar learning curve as the source company, then it will proceed down the curve in a similar way as is illustrated in Figure 7.8. Note that the area between the destination company curve and the source company curve represents the additional learning cost compared to the situation where the source company had continued production.

Thus, there will always be a loss of efficiency at the point of transfer because the destination company will start further back on the learning curve. In addition, it should be noted that errors are human and will always occur but that the rate of errors when a technology is newly transferred is likely to be higher than under normal circumstances. This is related to the knowledge at the destination company about the methods and procedures at the source company; see section *Information Sharing*. If there are different production philosophies, or if the knowledge about processes and methods used at the source company is relatively low at the destination company, there is a high probability that employees at the destination company will interpret the documentation incorrectly. These errors tend to diminish as the destination company becomes more familiar with the methods and processes of the source company. Training or technical assistance can also limit erroneous interpretations. The implication of the learning curve is that there will always be an initial loss of efficiency when a technology is transferred. This represents a *loss of learning* that diminishes as the destination company achieves a stabilized production line. However, as was discussed in section *Plant Location* in Chapter 5, it is quite possible that there are permanent differences in labor productivity, for example, the number of labor hours required to produce a product.

Environmental Factors

Three groups of environmental factors exist: national environmental factors, national business environmental factors, and industry environmental factors. National environmental factors were to some extend already discussed in Chapters 2 to 4 and are as follows:

- The political situation (international political position and the internal political stability) is a very important factor in technology transfer. It affects the travel possibilities and the ease of providing technical assistance and training. A politically unstable situation represents a risk to the source company. For a technology sale, such as in the first case, risk is connected with payments. This risk can be decreased by the source company demanding bank guarantees from the destination company. In cases where a technology is shared with a supplier, as in the second, third, and fourth case, risk is related to the ability of the destination company to meet the production schedule. It is difficult to hedge against this risk unless the source company uses a multiple source strategy.

- The economic situation concerns the type of economy (e.g., market economy or planned economy). It provides an insight on the ease of importing and exporting goods, and on the decision-making power and the length of the decision-making process. The condition of the economy is also a factor of the economic situation. It indicates the availability of financial means (especially relevant for state-owned companies), and the ability to generate income, which reflects the productivity level of a country.

- The level of industrialization (the infrastructure, especially communication infrastructure and the level of education) has impact on the transfer of a production technology. This goes back to the discussion from Chapter 3 and also section *Input Conditions* in Chapter 4. As Figure 7.4 illustrates, a production technology cannot simply be removed from the source company and placed at a destination company. The production technology is not independent of the organization and its environment. The level of industrialization is a particularly important variable in a technology transfer between a source company in an industrially developed country and a destination company in an industrially developing country. As discussed in section *Input Conditions* in Chapter 4, an underdeveloped infrastructure and a poor educational system in a destination country often leads to problems with production.

Furthermore, there is a high probability that the time (from ordering materials to finished product) for producing a part in an industrially developing country is longer than that required in an industrially developed country.

- The national culture affects the time required to accomplish a specific task. An important variable in this regard is the attitude toward time; see also Chapter 2 with the discussion of multiactive cultures. In countries where the national attitude toward time is relaxed, the efficiency will be low.
- The working conditions are a final important factor of the national environment. In poor working conditions, the employees will be less able to do a particular job. This results in mistakes and extended time required to finish the work.

The national business environment factors concern the level of related industries related to the level of industrialization. For a low level, a choice can be made to either import materials and parts or to develop the local industries. Developing local industries requires time and is expensive. A low industrialization level increases the cost of materials and parts.

The industry environmental factors are related to the overall level of development of the country (Chapter 4) and also relate to the industrial commons (see Chapter 3):

- The level of concentration in the industry that gives an indication of the fierceness of competition between rival companies. Competition may lead to innovative behavior and result in process and product improvements. Alternatively, if the situation in the destination country is not characterized by competition, then there may be less incentive to innovate.
- The strategic position of the organization in the industry is linked to the level of concentration in the industry. The strategic position in the industry influences whether or not a company can obtain more than average returns on investment. The strategic position also gives an indication of the bargaining power of the companies. This plays a role in, for example, instances where the destination company is a supplier to the source company.

- The mandatory requirements in the industry. For example, for aviation, there is a requirement for aircraft certification as well as production organization certification. This has been one of the most challenging areas to develop. Even Japan, which is currently developing a regional jet aircraft, is facing challenges with creating these organizational structures. The point here is that regardless of how well established a destination company is in its own environment, it must in this case abide by more global rules. Where cooperation has not occurred in the past, it often is a cumbersome process that takes a lot of time and resources.

- The demand for the final product is another important factor. It is only (economically) sensible to produce a product if there is a demand for it. Fluctuations in demand affect the production rates of the final product as well as the parts and this affects the rates across the international operations network, for example, in other offshore or source plants. In addition to the real market demand, the switch from dual sources to a single source also affects the schedule. Complicating this matter is what happens at the source that is not being used anymore. For example, consider a situation where a dual source strategy is used but where the first source (e.g., a source plant) is used to train employees at the second source (e.g., a lower cost offshore plant) so that the second source will eventually become the single source. If the plan is to close the plant and lay-off the employees after training has been completed, then there might be opposition to this from the workforce. An uncooperative workforce in this regard will influence the ability to transfer production to the second plant.

Activities When Installing a Technology

Figure 7.5 illustrates how the transfer of technology contains three sequential phases: preparation, installation, and utilization. During the preparation phase, the companies are involved in a dialogue where they estimate and decide on the type of technology that will be transferred, how to schedule it, and so forth. The last phase, utilization, is when the production technology is functioning at the new plant location. Note that this may be at a lower level of productivity than at plant where the production was initially located as discussed in previous chapters. Main activities at this point are: ramping-up the production, which is affected by the learning curve, dealing with technical problems, managing the continuous production, and managing the international operations network.

Let us look a little bit closer at the middle phase, that is the installation. This is where technology is actually being transferred. Understanding what needs to take place here will allow insight into possible cost of the transfer. Note that if it is determined that it is better to continue production at another plant or location because it is, for example, estimated that the production cost in that location is lower, then it still does not mean that production should be transferred. This depends on the cost involved in the actual transfer and whether the benefits of the new plant location compensate for the cost of the transfer. Figure 7.9 illustrates the transfer process.

The installation phase contains five groups of activities. Typically, the first activity is the transfer of information to the destination company. This means, for example, drawings, process planning sheets, process specifications, bill of materials, and quality requirements. These documentations describe the production process and the requirements involved. Depending on the size of the technology, the cost of shipping this information can be substantial although in electronic format this can be reduced.

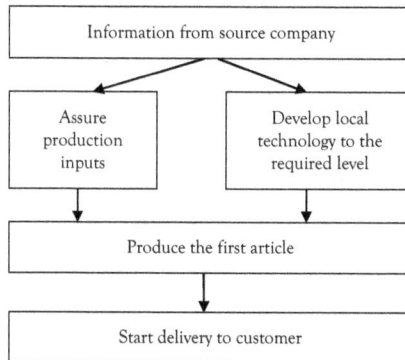

Figure 7.9 Installing the production technology, that is, the actual transfer

Source: Adapted from Steenhuis and de Bruijn (2003).

The second group of activities involves the development of technology at the required level. This goes back to Figure 7.6 and getting each of the components of technology up to the right level. People (humanware) may have to be hired and trained. It may also be necessary to have expatriates located at the site to provide assistance. As mentioned in Chapter 2, if the plant is located in a different culture, there may be an increased need for coordination and a permanent foreign expatriate might be required, that is, even in the continuous production stage. The factory and machines need to be brought in accordance with the technology requirements. For example, there may be strict requirements for temperature control, size of the factory, specifications for certain machines, and so forth. Tools such as jigs may have to be built or purchased or transferred from other plants. Especially if the tools are large and heavy, this may represent substantial cost. Probably the most underestimated technology component is the information aspect. This means that knowledge and understanding of the production processes has to be embedded at the new plant. Challenges with this will be discussed in section *Information Sharing*.

The third group of activities relates to making sure that inputs are available for the production process. This may involve developing local suppliers, purchasing materials, supplies, and so forth. In some instances, the local availability and quality may not be sufficient and it has to be imported from elsewhere. This can result in a higher cost for materials than in the original plant due to additional transportation cost and possibly tariffs that are applied.

The next group of activities relates to producing the first article. In terms of quality control and capability of the production process, this is a milestone achievement because the first article demonstrates that the plant is capable of the production. After the successful completion and inspection of the first article, deliveries to the customer can take place. Knudsen and Madsen (2014) provide additional insight into the management issues of the transfer and how this changes from operations management to project management during this installation stage as well as the challenges with a ramp-up and closing of the original location.

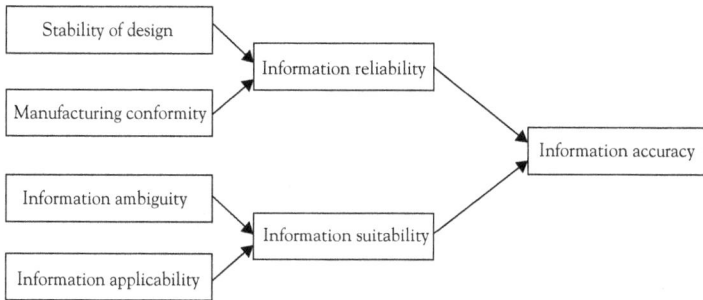

Figure 7.10 Information accuracy

Source: Based on Steenhuis and de Bruijn (2004b).

Information Sharing

As indicated in the opening example of this chapter, there often are issues with the accuracy of the information (Steenhuis and de Bruijn 2004b). Information accuracy relates to its reliability, that is, in absolute terms how good the information is at the source company, and its suitability, that is, in relative terms whether the destination company can use it, see Figure 7.10. As was explained earlier in this chapter, the reliability of information depends on the stability of the design and the manufacturing conformity—both are dependent upon age. Suitability of information depends on whether the information is ambiguous and whether it is applicable, as will be explained in the following text.

Information may not be applicable because different production philosophies are used, for example, using a lower degree of automation. An example of this was a company that used an automated riveting process for riveting parts together but transferred the production to a company that used a less automated process. The design for the automated riveting process essentially includes the software program for the machines, which indicates where rivets need to be placed. However, this software could not be used in the less automated situation. Consequently, the software program had to be converted into drawings with the exact location of the rivets so that operators could determine where to place rivets based on these drawings.

Information may also be ambiguous, that is, open to different interpretations, and people are often not aware of this. This is because systems used for codifying information may be different between different plants so that what appears similar may actually represent different things. An example of this was a situation of outsourcing that included a drawing with a hole that seemed to be in the wrong spot. The new supplier relied heavily on engineering and this meant that drawings were not questioned. The customer, that is the organization where the production had originally taken place and that supplied the drawing to the new supplier, did not have this approach. Instead, people had been trained to look at the right side of the drawing for confirmation when differences between the left side and the right side were observed in drawings where similarities were expected. Hence, the product was produced by the new supplier with a hole in the wrong location. On hindsight, this is easily explained and could have been avoided but the problem is that there was no awareness of it. In both organizations it is considered a *no-brainer* to produce according to the drawing (one plant) or to look at the right side of the drawing (the other plant).

Several other characteristics play a role in the ability to transfer know-how across plants. Ferdows (2006) identified two main characteristics, that is, form of production know-how (tacit or codified) and the speed of change of the production know-how (slow or fast). Based on this he argues that slow and codified information can be transferred through manuals and systems, slow and tacit knowledge should be transferred by moving people, fast and codified through joint development, and fast and tacit through projects. Chai, Gregory, and Shi (2003) provide similar insights that connect how the knowledge can be transferred with different approaches such as training, and so forth. Note that the example at the beginning of this chapter and Figure 7.10 relate to codified information but that case problems still arose.

Estimating the Cost and Time of Transferring on Production Operations

This chapter has shown that transferring operations to another location can be rather complex. The main point to take away is that the awareness of the factors that influence the transfer in terms of cost and time can help managers to make better informed international operation decisions related to whether their company should really consider going international. To gain insight and sensitivity in the influence of national culture on production processes, a manager can do the following:

- First, it is important to understand how the domestic production processes have been embedded in, and therefore have been influenced by, the domestic environment. To determine this, it is necessary to gain in-depth insight into the technology, the organization, and the overall business environment. This chapter has provided the basics. Then, the manager needs to determine how this environment has influenced the production processes. For example, how information is codified and what is tacit, what kind of organization systems are used, and so forth.

- Next, the manager needs to identify the international host environment in terms of technology, organization, and the overall business environment. This is in particular important if the technology is transferred to an existing party such as when a company is acquired or when a joint venture is used.

- Once the environment of the domestic location as well as the international location is understood and their differences are identified, the scale of these differences need to be estimated and a plan for transfer needs to be formulated; see Figure 7.9 for a rough idea. Aspects that require special attention are the learning curve and how this affects setting up the production operations, and the accuracy of the information and how to deal with the inaccuracies.

- Lastly, the cost and time of the transfer needs to be estimated. Costs that might be included are the costs related to loss of productivity in terms of the learning curve, training cost, translation cost, shipping cost, downtime during the first article production due to solving of technical questions, and so forth. In terms of the time for transfer, this is related to the learning curve as well as general notions of how long it takes to ship items, translate documents, train people, and so forth.

Estimating the impact of the cost and time for transferring production operations is necessary and important because this is an area that is often underestimated. Furthermore, it connects with the discussion in Chapter 4 and some of the factors not only influence the one-time transfer but also the continuous operations.

Conclusion

This chapter illustrated some of the challenges with transferring manufacturing operations to other locations. Part of the difficulty with this transfer is that technology should not be viewed as independent upon its environment. Technology develops over time in specific circumstances, which influence its characteristics, such as how drawings are designed, how production processes are specified, and so forth. When manufacturing operations are transferred to another location, there is an initial loss of productivity due to the learning curve effect, that is, the new plant has to learn how to produce. In addition, there might be lasting effects of lower productivity due to the overall environment, that is, infrastructure, working conditions, and so forth. But what matters most for the successful transfer is that the new plant learns how to produce. This requires the absorption of documentation, skills, or both that may be transferred through training and assistance. Depending upon the type and size of technology and the local culture, this may require substantial resources, for example, many man hours in training and permanent foreign expatriates. In addition, there is cost for shipping documentation and transporting people. Apart from that, supply networks may have to be locally established and in developing nations they may not be of sufficient quantity and quality leading to a need to import with higher cost. Even if production at another plant is considered to be beneficial, one should carefully consider the cost and effort involved to transfer the manufacturing to determine its impact on the overall benefits.

CHAPTER 8

Conclusion

Many companies, whether they desire it or not, are faced with operating in an international environment. In this book, I have discussed international operations from a perspective of productivity. There are many different ways in which companies can be internationally engaged. Some, such as exports, are relatively simple while others, such as controlling an international operations network with a variety of plants with a variety of roles, can be very complex. In many instances, companies are not as successful, that is, productive, as they could be or expect to be. Often this relates to inadequate preparation ahead of time, for example, entering a foreign market with products that do not align with the culture of that market. In this book I have provided a discussion of topics, with many examples, that should help with a better preparation. The discussion followed the sequence as shown in Figure 8.1. Here I will draw some main conclusions from this discussion.

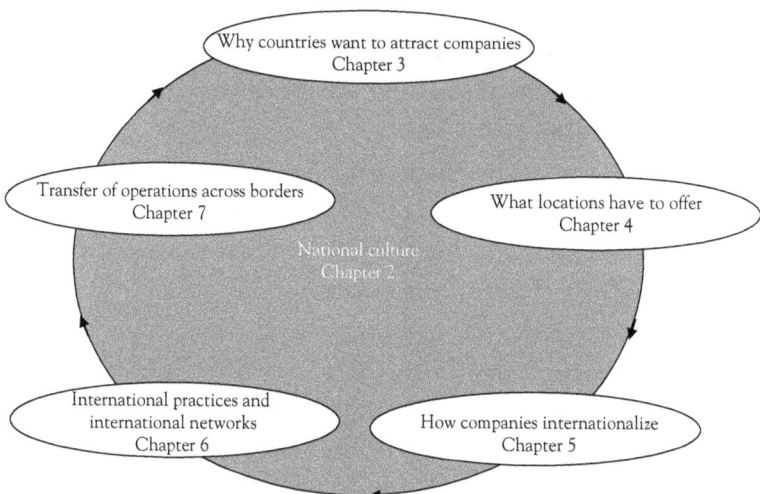

Figure 8.1 International operations

One of the most important and prominent issues in international operations is the national culture. National cultures affect business in many different ways, for example, in preferences of customers, and in the way products are promoted and produced. It is therefore important for a company to conduct a detailed analysis of national cultures and determine their affect. This relates to issues such as how to behave and what to expect at business meetings, determining what is legal and what might not be legal. For the sales of products in new overseas markets, it is critical to have an in-depth understanding of cultural differences in sales in international markets. Similarly, it is important to understand the culture of employees as this may affect their productivity. It is not unusual to find that in developing nations five or more times the employees need to be assigned for production compared to developed nations. Products and production technologies may have to be adapted to local circumstances, but it is unwise to do so ahead of time. One of the biggest challenges is communicating and working with people from other cultures, in particular when they have different ideas about time and organization. This is an aspect that is unlikely to change so instead should be incorporated into plans and associated costs, for example, the need for supervision.

In particular governments of developing countries are often eager to attract businesses and may even offer incentives such as reduced tax rates. Before companies jump on these offers, they need to examine the motives behind these incentives. An important analysis to conduct is to determine the type of economy of the country because this can provide valuable insight into overall levels of productivity. In many instances, governments are interested in attracting international businesses because these businesses are expected to enhance the environment. Hence, this also points out the weaknesses of those environments and businesses need to determine the cost and potential loss of productivity due to those weaknesses. Industry characteristics such as dependency upon the overall environment or upon other industries should be considered to determine the risks and costs. What this also means is that an estimate needs to be made whether the environment has the capacity to absorb the operations from the company and if not how long it would take to develop this capacity and the cost associated with it.

Discovering the potential of sales in international markets can be very exciting but an important part of the analysis is to look carefully at the *true* market size. Average incomes are not meaningful in many countries due to uneven income distribution. Similarly, population distributions should be considered for determining workforce size. Particular resources such as the global competitiveness report can provide many important insights with regard to the overall productivity level of a country and whether it has, for example, an infrastructure that is sufficiently developed, a workforce that is sufficiently educated, and whether it is subject to high levels of corruption. For instance, corruption may not only influence the cost of doing business, but it can also have an impact on lead times. In general, what should be kept in mind when operating internationally is that there are additional risks compared to only operating in the domestic situation. These risks relate to exposure to exchange rate fluctuations, exposure to possible corruption, supply chain risks, reputations risks, and so forth.

When companies, considering the preceding, have decided to get internationally involved, they can do so in many different ways and there is not one set sequence of doing so. The increased transportation and communication abilities have enabled companies to engage in international operations from their inception. Whether the company has ownership, internalization, and locational advantages should be carefully considered to determine the most appropriate channel for international engagement. Cost and issues of control also play a role. One approach that is often used and claimed to have large financial benefits is international outsourcing. However, scientific studies have pointed out that outsourcing is typically not a strategic approach and other approaches toward improving operations can lead to better results. Cost benefits are also not always achieved because of complicating factors such as labor productivity, and the increased need for communication and coordination. It is also important to use the right accounting information before a decision is made because overhead allocations and plant utilization can create additional complexities.

In particular for international manufacturing, it has been found that national environments influence how companies operate. Practices may not easily transfer to other countries, which relates to overall productivity levels. A careful analysis should be conducted to determine whether approaches, practices, and leadership techniques can be applied in another location and what their effect on productivity is. For example, a participatory leadership style may not work in some countries although countries may be able to achieve similar levels of productivity with other leadership styles. This also means that if expatriates are involved, then they should be carefully selected based on their ability to adjust to local circumstances. When considering multiple plants, there are several different international operations network approaches that can be applied. The type of network used depends on the one hand on the need to concentrate production due to production costs and on the other hand on the need to concentrate production due to transaction cost in relationship to market proximity. Within an international operations network, plants play different roles depending on the primary motive for the plant. Plants that are primarily established for cost reasons tend to be the least stable.

Even if the previous analysis shows that it is beneficial to locate production in another country, before a final decision can be made, it is necessary to determine the resources and time that it takes to transfer the operations. Part of the difficulty is that production technologies are not independent upon the environment but that these dependencies are often overlooked. For example, there are often problems with the transfer of know-how and embedding it in the new location. Furthermore, if production is transferred to another company and the original factory is going to be closed then there might be complications with training and assistance at the new organization by employees from the original plant because these employees might have low morale to help others while they are possibly losing their jobs after the training is completed. Technologies might not function well in other environments, machines might have to be imported, the supply chain might not be fully developed, and thus parts may have to be imported, and so forth. All in all, it is not trivial that a transfer leads into similar levels of productivity and transfers can be costly and time-consuming.

Nevertheless, when companies are well-prepared, they get to reap the benefits and joys of operating in international environments. In many instances, this enhances their competitive position because lessons learned

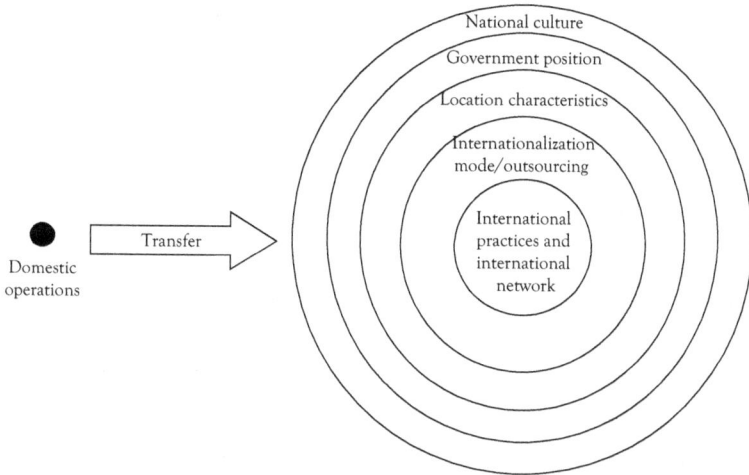

Figure 8.2 A model for analyzing international operations

from across the world can enhance their overall innovativeness and improvements and as a result increase their overall productivity.

Figure 8.2 summarizes the discussion and provides an overall model that operation managers can apply when they are considering to internationalize.

The model illustrates that to aid the decision-making process, by moving from the larger to the smaller circles and then the transfer arrow, a manager can do the following:

- Determine the differences in national culture between the domestic home country and the international host country and determine how the differences influence operations in terms of productivity overall (effectiveness and efficiency) related to both cost and timeliness of operations.
- Determine the host government position, that is, is it trying to attract the company? If so, why? What does that show about weaknesses of that country that may affect operations? Is the government willing to *pay* for the company to establish itself? And, what is the overall bargaining position of the government? In addition, is the company in an island industry or an integrated industry? An island industry can be more easily

developed in another location because it is less dependent upon other industries.

- Determine the general environment conditions. Environmental characteristics such as age group distribution and income distribution provide important clues for market potential. For production operations in particular, it is important to gain insight into how the overall environment affects the productivity. These environmental factors are more or less stable and thus have an impact on the productivity of continuous operations.

- Determine the channel used for internationalization. Different channels offer different degrees of control and cost of control. In particular for outsourcing, it is extremely important to consider whether it is strategic or tactical in nature. For the financial analysis, it is essential to include a broad range of issues and their cost for a more complete picture and to avoid making the wrong decision. Items such as more communication required, longer logistical pipelines, higher required inventory levels, the exposure to exchange rate fluctuations, and the financial impact on related remaining domestic operations should all be considered.

- Determine the differences in practices such as inventory control, management and leadership, and method of organizing. This is often overlooked because these practices are so common in particular locations, taught in institutes of education, and thus implicitly assumed to be the same across (international) locations. However, this is not the case and to change the mindset, regardless of which practices are ultimately applied, requires time and effort. In addition, the optimal operations network configuration based upon the product, market, and production characteristics, as well as the specific role of the plant, within the overall network needs to be determined. In light of changing international economic conditions, this should frequently be reassessed because, for instance, markets and labor costs develop over time.

- Determine the differences in the production environments by analyzing technology components, organization systems, and the general business environment. These differences provide insight into the cost and time required for transferring technology to international locations, as depicted through the arrow in Figure 8.2. The cost and time have aspects that are nonrecurring and happen for the first article inspection, for example, translating documents, but can also contain recurring elements such as a lower productivity due to learning curve differences.

There is not one prescribed method to deal with all of the complexities in international operations. The goal of the model in Figure 8.2 is to create awareness of these complexities so that better (strategic) decisions can be made for international operations and the location of the operations. Following the earlier steps, which have been discussed in more detail in previous chapters, allows managers to gain comprehensive and in-depth insight into the broad range of factors that play a role in international operations, thereby reducing the probability that critical mistakes are made in the decision-making process.

References

Abele, A., T. Meyer, U. Näher, G. Strube, and R. Sykes. 2008. *Global Production: A Handbook for Strategy and Implementation.* Berlin, Germany: Springer-Verlag.

Acosta, C., V.J. Leon, C. Conrad, R. Gonzalez, and C.O. Malave. 2004. "Case Study on Culture and Implementation of Manufacturing Strategy in Mexico." *Journal of Manufacturing Systems* 23, no. 3, pp. 204–14.

Asheim, B., P. Cooke, and R. Martin. 2006. "The Rise of the Cluster Concept in Regional Analysis and Policy, a Critical Assessment." In *Clusters and Regional Development, Critical Reflections and Explorations*, eds. B. Asheim, P. Cooke, and R. Martin. London, UK: Routledge.

Baranson, J. 1967. *Manufacturing Problems in India: The Cummins Diesel Experience.* Syracuse, New York: Syracuse University Press.

Bartlett, C.A., and S. Ghoshal. 2002. *Managing Across Borders: The Transnational Solution.* 2nd ed. Boston, MA: Harvard Business School Press.

Behrman, J.N., and H.W. Wallender. 1976. *Transfers of Manufacturing Technology within Multinational Enterprises.* Cambridge, MA: Ballinger Publishing Company.

Benito, G.R.G. 1997. "Divestment of Foreign Production Operations." *Applied Economics* 29, no. 10, pp. 1365–77.

Bernstein, W.J. 2004. *The Birth of Plenty: How the Prosperity of the Modern World was Created.* New York: McGraw-Hill.

Blair, J.P., and R. Premus. 1987. "Major Factors in Industrial Location: A Review." *Economic Development Quarterly* 1, no. 1, pp. 72–85.

Borrus, M. 1997. "Left for Dead: Asian Production Networks and the Revival of US Electronics." *Berkeley Roundtable on the International Economy Working Paper No. 100.* Berkeley, CA: University of California.

Boulaksil, Y., and J.C. Fransoo. 2010. "Implications of Outsourcing on Operations Planning: Findings from the Pharmaceutical Industry." *International Journal of Operations and Production Management* 30, no. 10, pp. 1059–79.

Bowonder, B., and T. Miyake. 1988. "Measurement of Technology at Industry Level: A Case Study of the Steel Industry in India and Japan." *Science and Public Policy* 15, no. 4, pp. 249–69.

Broedner, P., S. Kinkel, and G. Lay. 2009. "Productivity Effects of Outsourcing, New Evidence on the Strategic Importance of Vertical Integration Decisions." *International Journal of Operations and Production Management* 29, no. 2, pp. 127–50.

Brush, T.H., C.A. Maritan, and A. Karnani. 1999. "The Plant Location Decision in Multinational Manufacturing Firms: An Empirical Analysis of International Business and Manufacturing Strategy Perspectives." *Production and Operations Management* 8, no. 2, pp. 109–32.

Caddick, J.R., and B.G. Dale. 1987. "Sourcing from Less Developed Countries: A Case Study." *Journal of Purchasing and Materials Management* 23, no. 3, pp. 17–23.

Camuffo, A., A. Furlan, P. Romano, and A. Vinelli. 2007. "Routes Toward Supplier and Production Network Internationalisation." *International Journal of Operations and Production Management* 27, no. 4, pp. 371–87.

Chai, K.H., M. Gregory, and Y. Shi. 2003. "Bridging Islands of Knowledge: A Framework of Knowledge Sharing Mechanisms." *International Journal of Technology Management* 25, no. 8, pp. 703–27.

Coe, N.M., P. Dicken, and M. Hess. 2008. "Introduction: Global Production Networks—Debates and Challenges." *Journal of Economic Geography* 8, no. 3, pp. 267–9.

Cohen, W.M., and D.A. Levinthal. 1990. "Absorptive Capacity: A New Perspective on Learning and Innovation." *Administrative Science Quarterly* 35, no. 1, pp. 128–52.

Crick, D. 2009. "The Internationalization of Born Global and International New Venture SMEs." *International Marketing Review* 26, no. 4/5, pp. 453–76.

Cyhn, J.W. 2002. *Technology Transfer and International Production, the Development of the Electronics Industry in Korea.* Cheltenham, UK: Edward Elgar Publishing Limited.

Dabhilkar, M., and L. Bengtsson. 2008. "Invest or Divest? On the Relative Improvement Potential in Outsourcing Manufacturing." *Production Planning and Control* 19, no. 3, pp. 212–28.

Dalgic, T., and R. Heijblom. 1996. "International Marketing Blunders Revisited—Some Lessons for Managers." *Journal of International Marketing* 4, no. 1, pp. 81–91.

Dalton, B.M. 2005. "Corruption in Cultural Context: Contradictions within the Korean Tradition." *Crime, Law and Social Change* 43, pp. 237–62.

Danielmeyer, H. 1997. "The Development of the Industrial Society." *European Review* 5, no. 4, pp. 371–81.

De Blij, H. 2009. *The Power of Place, Geography, Destiny, and Globalization's Rough Landscape.* Oxford, UK: Oxford University Press.

Dekkers, R. 2011. "Impact of Strategic Decision Making for Outsourcing on Managing Manufacturing." *International Journal of Operations and Production Management* 31, no. 9, pp. 935–65.

Dolnicar, S., and B. Grun. 2007. "Cross-Cultural Differences in Survey Response Patterns." *International Marketing Review* 24, no. 2, pp. 127–43.

Dunning, J.H. 2000. "The Eclectic Paradigm as an Envelope for Economic and Business Theories of MNE Activity." *International Business Review* 9, no. 2, pp. 163–90.

Ferdows, K. 1997a. "Made in the World: The Global Spread of Production." *Production and Operations Management* 6, no. 2, pp. 102–9.

Ferdows, K. 1997b, "Making the Most of Foreign Factories." *Harvard Business Review,* March-April, pp. 73–88.

Ferdows, K. 1989. "Mapping International Factory Networks." In *Managing International Manufacturing,* ed. K. Ferdows, 3–21. Amsterdam, the Netherlands: North-Holland.

Ferdows, K. 2006. "Transfer of Changing Production Know-How." *Production and Operations Management* 15, no. 1, pp. 1–9.

Ferguson, N. 2011. *Civilization: The West and the Rest.* New York: The Penguin Press.

Flaherty, T. 1989. "International Sourcing: Beyond Catalog Shopping and Franchising." In *Managing International Manufacturing,* ed. K. Ferdows, Amsterdam, the Netherlands: North Holland.

Fleck, S.E. 2009. "International Comparisons of Hours Worked: An Assessment of the Statistics." *Monthly Labor Review* 132, no. 5, pp. 3–31.

Gannon, M.J., and R.K. Pillai. 2012. *Understanding Global Cultures, Metaphorical Journeys Through 31 Nations, Clusters of Nations, Continents, and Diversity.* 5th ed. Los Angeles, CA: Sage Publications.

Gereffi, G. 1999. "International Trade and Industrial Upgrading in the Apparel Commodity Chain." *Journal of International Economics* 48, no. 1, pp. 37–70.

Görg, H., A. Hanley, and E. Strobl. 2008. "Productivity Effects of International Outsourcing: Evidence from Plant-Level Data." *Canadian Journal of Economics* 41, no. 2, pp. 670–88.

Grant, E. 1999. *Fitness for Transfer: Assessing Manufacturing Technologies for Relocation.* Cambridge, UK: Cambridge University.

Harzing, A.W. 2006. "Response Styles in Cross-National Survey Research: A 26-Country Study." *International Journal of Cross-Cultural Management* 6, no. 2, pp. 243–66.

Hasselt, R. van, E.J. de Bruijn, and S.H. Wirjomartono. 1977. "An Investigation into the Appropriate Application of Modern Methods of Production and Management in the Engineering Industry of Indonesia." *Annals of CIRP* 25, no. 1, pp. 263–8.

Herron, C. and C. Hicks 2008. "The transfer of selected lean manufacturing techniques from Japanese automotive manufacturing into general manufacturing (UK) through change agents." *Robotics and Computer-Integrated Manufacturing* 24, pp. 524–531.

Hofstede, G. 1997. *Cultures and Organizations, Software of the Mind, Intercultural Cooperation and its Importance for Survival*. New York: McGraw-Hill.

Hofstede, G., B. Neuijen, D. Daval Ohayv, and G. Sanders. 1990. "Measuring Organizational Cultures: A Qualitative and Quantitative Study Across Twenty Cases." *Administrative Science Quarterly* 35, pp. 286–316.

Hofstede, G., G.J. Hofstede, and M. Minkov. 2010. *Cultures and Organizations, Software of the Mind, Intercultural Cooperation and Its Importance for Survival*. 3rd ed. New York: McGraw-Hill.

Hsiung, L.C. *Small and Medium Scale Enterprises—Development and Changes in Strategy, A Case Study of the Taiwanese Shoe Industry* [PhD dissertation]. The Netherlands: University of Twente; 1998.

Ietto-Gillies, G. 1992. *International Production, Trends, Theories, Effects*. Cambridge, UK: Polity Press.

Irawati, D., and D. Charles. 2010. "The Involvement of Japanese MNEs in the Indonesian Automotive Cluster." *International Journal of Automotive Technology and Management* 10, no. 2/3, pp. 180–96.

Jabar, J., C. Soosay, and R. Santa. 2011. "Organisational Learning as an Antecedent of Technology Transfer and New Product Development, A study of Manufacturing Firms in Malaysia." *Journal of Manufacturing Technology Management* 22, no. 1, pp. 25–45.

Jahns, C., E. Hartmann, and L. Bals. 2006. "Offshoring: Dimensions and Diffusion of a New Business Concept." *Journal of Purchasing and Supply Management* 12, no. 4, pp. 218–31.

Jarboe, K.P. 1986. "Location Decisions of High-Technology Firms: A Case Study." *Technovation* 4, no. 2, pp. 117–29.

Jia, X. *Creating Sino-Foreign Equity Joint Ventures* [PhD dissertation]. The Netherlands: University of Twente; 1993.

Kaufmann, D., and P.C. Vicente. 2011. "Legal Corruption." *Economics and Politics* 23, no. 2, pp. 195–219.

Ketels, C.H.M., and O. Memedovic. 2008. "From Clusters to Cluster-Based Economic Development." *International Journal of Technological Learning, Innovation and Development* 1, no. 3, pp. 375–92.

Khurana, A., and B. Talbot. 1998. "The Internationalization Process Model through the Lens of the Global Color Picture Tube Industry." *Journal of Operations Management* 16, no. 2, pp. 215–39.

Kinkel, S. 2012. "Trends in Production Relocation and Backshoring Activities, Changing Patterns in the Course of the Global Economic Crisis." *International Journal of Operations and Production Management* 32, no. 6, pp. 696–720.

Kitcher, B., I.P. McCarthy, S. Turner, and K. Ridgway. 2013. "Understanding the Effects of Outsourcing: Unpacking the Total Factor Productivity Variable." *Production Planning and Control* 24, no. 4/5, pp. 308–17.

Kleef, J. van. 2010. "Fast Food, Fast Money." *Quote* September, pp. 72–81.

Knight, G., T.K. Madson, and P. Servais. 2004. "An Inquiry into Born-Global Firms in Europe and the USA." *International Marketing Review* 21, no. 6, pp. 645–65.

Knudsen, M.P and E.S. Madsen 2014. "The managerial issues related to transferring shop floor knowledge in manufacturing relocation." *International Journal of Operations and Production Management* 34, no. 11, pp. 1389–1416.

Kotabe, M. 1989. "'Hollowing-Out'of U.S. Multinationals and their Global Competitiveness." *Journal of Business Research* 19, pp. 1–15.

Lane, C., and J. Probert. 2006. "Domestic Capabilities and Global Production Networks in the Clothing Industry: A Comparison of German and UK firms' Strategies." *Socio-Economic Review* 4, pp. 35–67.

Lee, K., and Lim, C. 2001. "Technological Regimes, Catching-Up and Leapfrogging: Findings from Korean Industries." *Research Policy* 30, pp. 459–83.

Lewis, R.D. 2008. *When Cultures Collide, Leading across Cultures: A Major New Edition of the Global Guide.* Boston, MA: Nicholas Brealey International.

Liemt, G. van 1992. *Industry on the Move: Causes and Consequences of International Relocation in the Manufacturing Industry.* Geneva, Switzerland: International Labour Office.

Lüthje, B. 2004. "Global Production Networks and Industrial Upgrading in China: The Case of Electronics Contract Manufacturing." *East-West Center Working Papers No. 74.* Honolulu, HI: East-West Center.

Mackintosh, J., and R. McGregor. 2003. "A Leap over the Cliff: Are the Big Profits to be Made in China Blinding Foreign Carmakers to the Risks Ahead?" *Financial Times*, August 25, pp. 13.

Maddison, A. 2006. *The World Economy.* Paris, France: OECD Publishing.

Mahajan, V. 2009. *Africa rising.* Upper Saddle River, New Jersey: Pearson Education, Inc.

Mahajan, V. 2012. *The Arab World Unbound.* San Francisco, CA: Jossey-Bass.

Marin, D., and M. Schnitzer. 1995. "Tying Trade Flows: A Theory of Countertrade with Evidence." *The American Economic Review* 85, no. 5, pp. 1047–64.

Markides, C.C., and N. Berg. 1988. "Manufacturing Offshore Is Bad Business, to Stay Competitive, Stay Home." *Harvard Business Review*, September-October, pp. 113–20.

Mason, R.H. 1981. "Comments on Alternative Channels and Modes of International Resource Transmission." In *Controlling International Technology Transfer, Issues, Perspectives, and Policy Implications*, eds. T. Sagafi-nejad, R.W. Moxon, and H.V. Perlmutter. New York: Pergamon Press.

Mazzarol, T., and S. Choo. 2003. "A Study of the Factors Influencing the Operating Location Decisions of Small Firms." *Property Management* 21, no. 2, pp. 190–208.

McCann, F. 2011. "The Heterogeneous Effect of International Outsourcing on Firm Productivity." *Review of World Economics* 147, no. 1, pp. 85–108.

Mefford, R.N. 1986. "Determinants of Productivity Differences in International Manufacturing." *Journal of International Business Studies* 17, no. 1, pp. 63–82.

Meixell, M.J., G.N. Kenyon, and P. Westfall. 2014. "The Effects of Production Outsourcing on Factory Cost Performance: An Empirical Study." *Journal of Manufacturing Technology Management* 25, no. 6, pp. 750–74.

Mitchell, B.R. 2007a. *International Historical Statistics, Africa, Asia and Oceania 1750–2005*. New York: Palgrave Macmillan.

Mitchell, B.R. 2007b. *International Historical Statistics, the Americas 1750–2005*. New York: Palgrave Macmillan.

Mitchell, B.R. 2007c. *International Historical Statistics, Europe 1750–2005*. New York: Palgrave Macmillan.

Morris, I. 2010. *Why the West Rules—for Now*. New York: Farrar, Straus and Giroux.

Morris, T., and C.M. Pavett. 1992. "Management Style and Productivity in Two Cultures." *Journal of International Business Studies* 23, no. 1, pp. 169–79.

Naser, K., A. Jamal, and K. Al-Khatib. 1999. "Islamic Banking: A Study of Customer Satisfaction and preferences in Jordan." *International Journal of Bank Marketing* 17, no. 3, pp.135–51.

O'Neill, J. 2011. *The Growth Map, Economic Opportunity in the BRICs and Beyond*. New York: Portfolio/Penguin.

Pagell, M., J.P. Katz, and C. Sheu. 2005. "The Importance of National Culture in Operations Management Research." *International Journal of Operations and Production Management* 25, no. 4, pp. 371–94.

Phillips, P.D. 1991. "Site Selection: Corporate Perspective and Community Response." *Economic Development Review* 9, no. 2, pp. 4–11.

Pisano, G.P., and W.C. Shih. 2009. "Restoring American Competitiveness." *Harvard Business Review*, July-August, pp. 114–25.

Porter, M.E. 1990. *The Competitive Advantage of Nations*. New York: The Free Press.

Porter, M.E. 2008. *On Competition*. Boston, MA: Harvard Business School Publishing.

Porter, M.E., C. Ketels, and M. Delgado. 2007. "The Microeconomic Foundations of Prosperity: Findings from the Business Competitiveness Index." In *The global Competitiveness Report 2007–2008*, eds. K. Schwab, and M.E. Porter, 51–81. New York: Palgrave Macmillan.

Premus, R. 1982. *Location of High Technology Firms and Regional Economic Development, A Staff Study Prepared for the Use of the Subcommittee on Monetary and Fiscal Policy of the Joint Economic Committee Congress of the United State.* Washington, DC: U.S. Government Printing Office.

Radelet, S. 2010. *Emerging Africa, How 17 countries are leading the way.* Washington DC: Center for Global Development.

Ramanathan, K. 1988. "Measurement of Technology at the Firm Level." *Science and Public Policy* 15, no. 4, pp. 230–48.

Ramanathan, K. 1994. "The Polytrophic Components of Manufacturing Technology." *Technological Forecasting and Social Change* 46, no. 3, pp. 221–58.

Rho, B.H., and D.C. Whybark. 1993. "Comparing Manufacturing Practices in the People's Republic of China and South Korea." In *Global Manufacturing Practices, A Worldwide Survey of Practices in Production Planning Control,* eds. D.C. Whybark, and G. Vastag. Amsterdam, the Netherlands: Elsevier.

Ricks, D.A. 1995. *Blunders in International Business.* Cambridge, MA: Blackwell Publishers

Sauian, M.S. 2002. "Labour Productivity: An Important Business Strategy in Manufacturing." *Integrated Manufacturing Systems* 13, no. 6, pp. 435–8.

Schwab, K., and X. Sala-i-Martín. 2013. *Global Competitiveness Report 2013–2014.* Geneva, Switzerland: World Economic Forum.

Schwab, K., M. Porter, J.D. Sachs, and A. Warner. 1999. *The Global Competitiveness Report 1999.* New York: Oxford University Press.

Sharif, M.N. 1988. "Basis for Techno-Economic Policy Analysis" *Science and Public Policy* 15, no. 4, pp. 217–29.

Shi, Y., and M. Gregory. 1998. "International Manufacturing Networks—To Develop Global Competitive Capabilities." *Journal of Operations Management* 16, no. 2, pp. 195–214.

Shin, S.J., F.P. Morgeson, and M.A. Campion. 2007. "What You Do Depends on Where You Are: Understanding How Domestic and Expatriate Work Requirements Depend Upon the Cultural Context." *Journal of International Business Studies* 38, no. 1, pp. 64–83.

Shurchuluu, P. 2002. "National Productivity and Competitive Strategies for the New Millennium." *Integrated Manufacturing Systems* 13, no. 6, pp. 408–14.

Song, N., K. Platts, and D. Bance. 2007. "Total Acquisition Cost of Overseas Outsourcing/Sourcing: A Framework and a Case Study." *Journal of Manufacturing Technology Management* 18, no. 7, pp. 858–75.

Steenhuis, H.J., and E.J. de Bruijn. 2001. "Evaluating International Transfer of Technology." *In Management of Technology: The Key to Prosperity in the Third*

Millennium, eds. T.M. Khalil, L.A. Lefebvre, and R.M. Mason. Amsterdam, the Netherlands: Pergamon.

Steenhuis, H.J., and E.J. de Bruijn. 2002. "Technology Transfer and Learning." *Technology Analysis and Strategic Management* 14, no. 1, pp. 57–66.

Steenhuis, H.J., and E.J. de Bruijn. 2003. "Implementing the International Relocation of Production Technology." *In Management of Technology: Growth through Business Innovation and Entrepreneurship,* eds. M. von Zedtwitz, G. Haour, T.M. Khalil, and L.A. Lefebvre. Amsterdam, the Netherlands: Pergamon.

Steenhuis, H.J., and, E.J. de Bruijn. 2004a. "Assessing Manufacturing Location." *Production Planning and Control* 15, no. 8, pp. 786–95.

Steenhuis, H.J., and E.J. de Bruijn. 2004b. "Exploring Knowledge Transfer within Manufacturing Networks and Codified Information Characteristics: The Hidden Dangers of Inaccurate Information." *International Journal of Technology Transfer and Commercialization* 3, no. 4, pp. 433–53.

Steenhuis, H.J., and E.J. de Bruijn. 2006. "International Shopfloor Level Productivity Differences: An Exploratory Study." *Journal of Manufacturing Technology Management* 17, no. 1, pp. 42–55.

Steenhuis, H.J., and E.J. de Bruijn. 2007. "Exploring the Impact of National Culture on the Outcome of International Technology Transfer Projects." *International Journal of Technology Transfer and Commercialization* 6, no. 2/3/4, pp. 212–34.

Stevenson, W.J. 2015. *Operations Management.* 12th ed. New York, NY: McGraw-Hill Education.

Štrach, P., and A.M. Everett. 2007. "International Manufacturing In/Divestment Strategy: Flextronics in the Czech Republic." *International Journal of Manufacturing Technology and Management* 11, no. 1, pp. 115–32.

Symons, M. 2005. *This Book of More Perfectly Useless Information.* New York: Harper Collins Publishers.

Szulanski, G., and R.J. Jensen. 2006. "Presumptive Adaptation and the Effectiveness of Knowledge Transfer." *Strategic Management Journal* 27, no. 10, pp. 937–57.

Tahir, R., and J. Larimo. 2004. "Understanding the Location Strategies of the European firms in Asian Countries." *Journal of American Academy of Business* 5, no. 1/2, pp. 102–9.

Taylor, B. 2001. "The Management of Labour in Japanese Manufacturing Plants in China." *International Journal of Human Resource Management* 12, no. 4, pp. 601–20.

Technology Atlas Team. 1987. "Components of Technology for Resources Transformation." *Technological Forecasting and Social Change* 32, no. 1, pp. 19–35.

Trent, R.J., and R.M. Monczka. 2003. "Understanding Integrated Global Sourcing." *International Journal of Physical Distribution and Logistics Management* 33, no. 7, pp. 607–29.

Triandis, H.C. 1994. *Culture and Social Behavior.* New York: McGraw-Hill.

Trompenaars, F., and C. Hampden-Turner. 2012. *Riding the Waves of Culture, Understanding Cultural Diversity in Busines.* 3rd ed. New York: McGraw-Hill.

U.S. International Trade Commission. 1998. *The Changing Structure of the Global Large Civil Aircraft Industry and Market: Implications for the Competitiveness of the U.S. Industry.* Washington DC: U.S. International Trade Commission.

Ulgado, F.M. 1996. "Location Characteristics of Manufacturing Investments in the U.S.: A Comparison of American and Foreign-Based Firms." *Management International Review* 36, no. 1, pp. 7–26.

United Nations 2013. *World Investment Report 2013, Global Value Chains: Investment and Trade for Development.* Geneva, Switzerland: United Nations.

Van Ark, B., and R.H. McGuckin. 1999. "International Comparisons of Labor Productivity and Per Capita Income." *Monthly Labor Review* 122, no. 7, pp. 33–41.

Van de Ven, A.D.M., and P.J.M. van Laarhoven. 1997. "Oost-West, Oost-Best?" *Internationaal ondernemen* 2, no. 1, pp. 15–21.

Veld, J. in't 1992. *Analyse Van Organisatie Problemen.* Leiden, Netherlands: Stenfert Kroese Uitgevers.

Vereecke, A., A. De Meyer, and R. Van Dierdonck. 2008. *The Strategic Role of the Plant in International Networks: A Longitudinal Study.* Working Paper, University of Gent. http://www.jbs.cam.ac.uk/fileadmin/user_upload/research/workingpapers/wp0809.pdf

Vereecke, A., and van R. Dierdonck. 2002. "The Strategic Role of the Plant: Testing Ferdows's model." *International Journal of Operations and Production Management* 22, no. 5/6, 492–514.

Vereecke, A., R. Van Dierdonck, and A. De Meyer. 2006. "A Typology of Plants in Global Manufacturing networks." *Management Science* 52, no. 11, pp. 1737–1750.

Vernon, R. 1966. "International Investment and International Trade in the Product Cycle." *The Quarterly Journal of Economics* 80, no. 2, pp. 190–207.

Vietor, R.H.K. 2007. *How Countries Compete, Strategy, Structure, and Government in the Global Economy.* Boston, MA: Harvard Business School Press.

Waiters, E. 2013. "We Aren't the World." *Pacific Standard,* March/April, pp. 46–53.

Whangthomkum, N., B. Igel, and M. Speece. 2006. "An Empirical Study of the Relationship Between Absorptive Capacity and Technology Transfer Effectiveness." *International Journal of Technology Transfer and Commercialization* 5, no. 1/2, pp. 31–55.

Whybark, D.C., and G. Vastag. 1993. *Global Manufacturing Practices: A Worldwide Survey of Practices in Production Planning Control.* Amsterdam, the Netherlands: Elsevier.

Williamson, J. 1990 *Latin American Adjustment: How Much Has to Happen.* Washington, DC: Peterson Institute for International Economics.

Wlazlak, P.G., and G. Johansson. 2014. "R&D in Sweden and Manufacturing in China: A Study of Communication Challenges." *Journal of Manufacturing Technology Management* 25, no. 2, pp. 258–78.

World Bank 2013. *World Development Report 2014: Risk and Opportunity— Managing Risk for Development.* Washington, DC: The World Bank.

Yang, C., J.G. Wacker, and C. Sheu. 2012. "What Makes Outsourcing Effective? A Transaction-Cost Economics Analysis." *International Journal of Production Research* 50, no. 16, pp. 4462–76.

Yokozawa, K., and H.J. Steenhuis. 2013. "The Influence of National Level Factors on International Kaizen Transfer, an Exploratory Study in the Netherlands." *Journal of Manufacturing Technology Management* 24, no. 7, pp. 1051–75.

Index

OTHER TITLES IN OUR SUPPLY AND OPERATIONS MANAGEMENT COLLECTION

Johnny Rungtusanatham, The Ohio State University, Editor

- *Global Supply Chain Management* by Matt Drake
- *Managing Commodity Price Risk: A Supply Chain Perspective* by George A. Zsidisin
- *Improving Business Performance With Lean* by James Bradley
- *RFID for the Supply Chain and Operations Professional* by Pamela Zelbst and Victor Sower
- *Insightful Quality: Beyond Continuous Improvement* by Victor Sower and Frank Fair
- *Sustainability Delivered: Designing Socially and Environmentally Responsible Supply Chains* by Madeleine Pullman and Margaret Sauter
- *Sustainable Operations and Closed-Loop Supply Chains* by Gilvan Souza
- *Mapping Workflows and Managing Knowledge: Capturing Formal and Tacit Knowledge to Improve Performance* by John Kmetz
- *Supply Chain Planning: Practical Frameworks for Superior Performance* by Matthew Liberatore and Tan Miller
- *Understanding the Dynamics of the Value Chain* by William Presutti and John Mawhinney
- *An Introduction to Supply Chain Management: A Global Supply Chain Support Perspective* by Edmund Prater and Kim Whitehead
- *Sourcing to Support the Green Initiative* by Lisa Ellram and Wendy Tate
- *Designing Supply Chains for New Product Development* by Antonio Arreola-Risa and Barry Keys
- *Metric Dashboards for Operations and Supply Chain Excellence* by Jaideep Motwani and Rob Ptacek
- *Statistical Process Control for Managers* by Victor E. Sower
- *Supply Chain Risk Management: Tools for Analysis, Second Edition* by David L. Olson

Announcing the Business Expert Press Digital Library

Concise e-books business students need for classroom and research

This book can also be purchased in an e-book collection by your library as

- a one-time purchase,
- that is owned forever,
- allows for simultaneous readers,
- has no restrictions on printing, and
- can be downloaded as PDFs from within the library community.

Our digital library collections are a great solution to beat the rising cost of textbooks. E-books can be loaded into their course management systems or onto students' e-book readers.
The **Business Expert Press** digital libraries are very affordable, with no obligation to buy in future years. For more information, please visit **www.businessexpertpress.com/librarians**. To set up a trial in the United States, please email **sales@businessexpertpress.com**.

www.ingramcontent.com/pod-product-compliance
Lightning Source LLC
Chambersburg PA
CBHW070919270326
41927CB00011B/2636